IN ASSOCIATION WITH
IMPERIAL WAR MUSEUMS

THE STORY OF
D-DAY

JUNE 6TH, 1944

THE ALLIED INVASION OF NORMANDY

RICHARD HOLMES

METRO BOOKS
New York

CONTENTS

METRO BOOKS
New York

An Imprint of Sterling Publishing Co., Inc.
1166 Avenue of the Americas
New York, NY 10036

METRO BOOKS and the distinctive Metro Books logo are trademarks of Sterling Publishing Co., Inc.

Design and maps © 2014 by Carlton Books Limited
Text © 2004 by Richard Holmes
IWM images © IWM, www.iwm.org.uk

ISBN 978-1-4351-5784-2

For information about custom editions, special sales, and premium and corporate purchases, please contact Sterling Special Sales at 800-805-5489 or specialsales@sterlingpublishing.com.

Manufactured in Dubai

2 4 6 8 10 9 7 5 3

www.sterlingpublishing.com

INTRODUCTION

It was the largest-ever amphibious operation, and is one of those events for which the much-misused phrase "turning point" is indeed appropriate.

Yet there is more to the summer of 1944 than D-Day, crucial though it was. First, we must acknowledge the role played by Russia in eating the heart out of the German army. D-Day is seen in its proper context only if set alongside the Russian Belorussian offensive, which destroyed German Army Group Centre on the Eastern Front.

Second, D-Day was made possible by the Western Allies' efforts elsewhere. Strategic bombing weakened the German industrial base and diverted resources to the defence of the Reich. The long and painful slog up Italy by the men nicknamed "D-Day dodgers" forced the Germans to commit troops who would have been valuable on the Eastern or Western fronts. Nor should we forget that while D-Day was the much-publicized beginning of the end of the war in Europe, in Burma Bill Slim's 14th Army battled on far from the spotlight.

D-Day also relied on naval superiority. Without the Battle of the Atlantic there could have been no D-Day. Though the emphasis of this book is on land operations in France, no historian can be unaware of the part played by the naval plan, Operation Neptune, in enabling the landings to take place. Almost 7,000 vessels, from battleships to landing craft, were assigned to Operation Neptune. Most were British, American and Canadian, but there were also French, Norwegian, Dutch, Polish and Greek vessels.

Last, D-Day's importance all too often obscures the significance of the Normandy campaign as a whole. Getting ashore was only part of the challenge. The force disembarked in Normandy had to be sustained with food, ammunition and reinforcements along sea lanes kept open by Allied navies, and supported by aircraft from strategic bombers to the Dakotas which helped revolutionize the evacuation of casualties. Many Normany veterans recall not the landing itself, but the fighting that followed. There was nothing easy in being an infantryman or tank crewman in Normany, some of those battles were attritional grinds. This is a book that looks at the campaign as a whole.

I have been a military historian most of my working life. When I first visited the D-Day beaches, most of the veterans I met on them were younger than I am now. There will be fewer veterans in Normandy this year, and fewer still next. Yet they lie at the very heart of my story. I grew up in the shadow of the Second World War, and take the view that it was not a struggle from which my father's generation could stand aside. It could, in common with most wars, have been foreseen with greater prescience, and prosecuted with greater efficiency. But my generation owes a lasting debt to the men and women whose sacrifices made Allied victory possible: this book, above all, is their story.

RICHARD HOLMES

INDEX OF MAPS

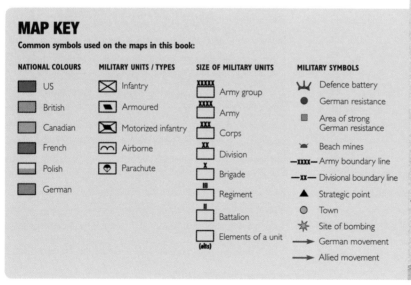

MAP KEY

Common symbols used on the maps in this book:

NATIONAL COLOURS
- US
- British
- Canadian
- French
- Polish
- German

MILITARY UNITS / TYPES
- ⊠ Infantry
- ◼ Armoured
- ⊠ Motorized infantry
- ⌢ Airborne
- ⬙ Parachute

SIZE OF MILITARY UNITS
- XXXXX Army group
- XXXX Army
- XXX Corps
- XX Division
- X Brigade
- III Regiment
- II Battalion
- Elements of a unit (elts)

MILITARY SYMBOLS
- ⩊ Defence battery
- ● German resistance
- ◼ Area of strong German resistance
- ⚓ Beach mines
- —XXXX— Army boundary line
- —XX— Divisional boundary line
- ▲ Strategic point
- ○ Town
- ✸ Site of bombing
- → German movement
- ➤ Allied movement

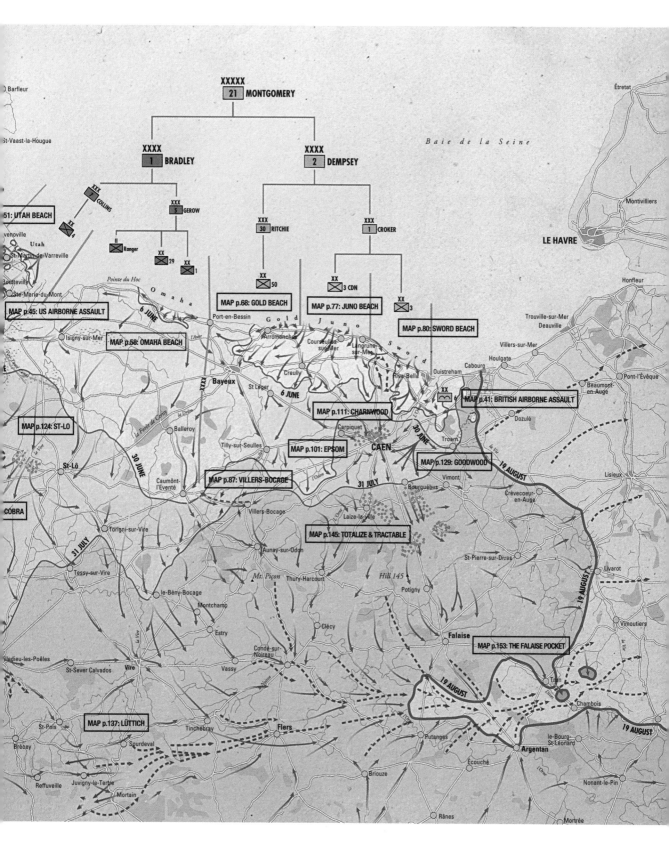

XXXXX
21 MONTGOMERY

XXXX
1 BRADLEY

XXXX
2 DEMPSEY

XXX COLLINS

XXX
5 GEROW

XXX
30 RITCHIE

XXX
1 CROKER

51: UTAH BEACH

XX
4

II Ranger

XX
29

XX
1

XX
50

XX
3 CDN

XX
3

Barfleur

St-Vaast-la-Hougue

Baie de la Seine

Étretat

Montivilliers

LE HAVRE

venoville

Utah

St-Martin-de-Varreville

Boutteville

Ste-Marie-du-Mont

Pointe du Hoc

Omaha

6 JUNE

Port-en-Bessin

Gold

Juno

Arromanches

Courseulles-sur-Mer

Langrune-sur-Mer

Sword

Honfleur

Trouville-sur-Mer
Deauville

Villers-sur-Mer

Houlgate

MAP p.45: US AIRBORNE ASSAULT

Isigny-sur-Mer

MAP p.58: OMAHA BEACH

l'Aure

Creully

St-Léger

6 JUNE

Riva-Bella

Ouistreham

Cabourg

Beaumont-en-Auge

Pont-l'Évêque

MAP p.68: GOLD BEACH

MAP p.77: JUNO BEACH

MAP p.80: SWORD BEACH

Bayeux

XXXX

la Forêt de Cérisy

la Drôme

MAP p.124: ST-LO

Balleroy

Tilly-sur-Seulles

MAP p.111: CHARNWOOD

Carpiquet

MAP p.101: EPSOM

CAEN

30 JUNE

Troarn

Dozulé

MAP p.41: BRITISH AIRBORNE ASSAULT

XX

Crèvecoeur-en-Auge

Lisieux

St-Lô

30 JUNE

Caumônt-l'Eventé

l'Odon

MAP p.87: VILLERS-BOCAGE

MAP p.129: GOODWOOD

Vimont

19 AUGUST

COBRA

Torigni-sur-Vire

Villers-Bocage

31 JULY

Bourguébus

Laize-la-Ville

Livarot

31 JULY

MAP p.145: TOTALIZE & TRACTABLE

St-Pierre-sur-Dives

Tessy-sur-Vire

Aunay-sur-Odon

le-Bény-Bocage

Mt. Piçon

Thury-Harcourt

Hill 145

Potigny

Vimoutiers

Montchamp

Clécy

19 AUGUST

illedieu-les-Poêles

St-Sever Calvados

Estry

Vire

Condé-sur-Noireau

Vassy

Falaise

MAP p.153: THE FALAISE POCKET

Trun

19 AUGUST

Chambois

MAP p.137: LÜTTICH

Tinchebray

Flers

19 AUGUST

19 AUGUST

St-Pois

Spurdeval

Putanges

le-Bourg-St-Léonard

Brécey

Ecouché

Argentan

Reffuveille

Juvigny-le-Tertre

Briouze

Nonant-le-Pin

Mortain

Rânes

Mortrée

THE PLANNING

On 12 February 1944 General Dwight D. Eisenhower, Supreme Commander, Allied Expeditionary Force, was directed to "enter the Continent of Europe and, in conjunction with other United Nations, undertake operations aimed at the heart of Germany and the destruction of her armed forces."

It had been clear from December 1941 that the defeat of Germany was the principal Allied war aim, although there were challenges to overcome before an invasion of Europe was possible. War industry had to be developed, and sea and air communications maintained: winning the Battle of the Atlantic against German submarines would be crucial. Germany was worn down by land, air and sea, with her industrial capacity eroded by the growing weight of Allied strategic bombing. The war against Japan forced America and, to a lesser degree, Britain, to devote resources to the Far East, and the relationship with Russia, whose leader Joseph Stalin repeatedly demanded the opening of a second front, had to be developed.

While the Allies were united in their opposition to Germany, they had practical and cultural differences. The British sometimes struck the Americans as over-cautious and preoccupied with imperial concerns, while the Americans sometimes seemed brash and headstrong. Nevertheless, there were sufficient good working relationships within the alliance, notably that between US President Franklin D. Roosevelt and British Prime Minister Winston Churchill, to ensure that strategy moved inexorably in the right direction.

ABOVE: Band of Brothers? The Allied commanders, 1 February 1944. From left to right: Bradley, Ramsay, Tedder, Eisenhower, Montgomery, Leigh-Mallory, and Eisenhower's chief of staff, Walter Bedell Smith.

RIGHT: Envelope used for circulating SHAEF meeting minutes.

OVERLEAF: German intelligence map issued on 3 July 1944. Thanks to Allied deception plans, the Germans hugely over-estimated the number of Allied divisions stationed in Britain.

21 AGP/1062/1/0=1o=2.

TOP SECRET

GARDD CONFIDENTIAL.

TO BE KEPT UNDER
LOCK AND KEY

It is requested that special care may be taken
to ensure the secrecy of this document.

Kräftegruppe Schottland
4.c.Armee (Schottland)
VII.e.A.K.
1.poln.A.K.
12.e.ᵗ, 52.e.Cdo.
55.a., 1.a.ᵗ.Btl.
2.poln/Pz.Gr.Div.
1.poln/F.S.Brig., 1.norw.Br., 1.norw.Btl.

Kräftegruppe Humber-Mündung
11.e.W.e.ᵗ
48.e., 62.e.ᵗ, 77.e.ᵗ,80.e.ᵗ/1.we.ᵗ,6.e.
20.e.H.Pz.Regt.ᵗ
1.poln.Pz.Div.ᵗ

Verbleib unbekannt, jedoch in Großbritannien/
Nordirland zu vermuten.
III.a.A.K.
9.e.ᵗ, 90.e.ᵗ.
1.ᵗ kan.Pz.Div.,99.e.
42.e.,44.e.,46.e., Cdo. 1.ᵗ kan. F.S.Brig
11.a.L.L.ᵗ

Erläuterung:

✪ = OKW. - Reserven
⬭ = Heeresgruppen-
◯ = Armee-
▣ = Korps-
▷ = engl.
▶ = amerik.
☆ = Festung

21.
Montgomery

1. Gen. Bradley

2. Gen. Anderson

Pz.Gr.West

le MAA 681

MA Rgt 1.
(MAA 683 + 608)

Tle MAA 681

Tle MAA 608

Geheime Kommandosache

Chef-Sache!
Nur durch Offizier!

Lage West
Stand: 3.7.44
OKH - Gen St d H
Op.Abt.IIIb PrüfNr.

Geo-Verlag K.G., Berlin 55

PARIS · Stadt von über 100 000 Einwohnern
LE HAVRE · Stadt von über 50 000 Einwohnern
CALAIS · Stadt von über 30 000 Einwohnern

Verdun · Stadt von über 10 000 Einwohnern
Bethel · Stadt von über 3 000 Einwohnern
Boudère · Ort von unter 3 000 Einwohnern
· Kleinerer Ort

Staatsgrenzen
Länder- und Reichsgaugrenzen im Deutschen Reich
Provinzgrenzen im Deutschen Reich

Regierungsbezirksgrenzen im Deutschen Reich,
Departementsgrenzen in Frankreich und
entsprechende Grenzen in den übrigen Staaten

Frankreich

Operation Bolero saw the concentration of US men and equipment in Britain. After the Allied invasion of North Africa in November 1942, an Allied conference at Casablanca outlined plans for the invasion of Europe in 1944. Although a Supreme Allied Commander was not yet nominated, the British Lieutenant General F. E. Morgan was appointed "Chief of Staff to the Supreme Allied Commander (designate)", Cossac for short. The Washington conference in May 1943 elaborated the forces that he would have at his disposal, and ordered that a draft of the plan for what was now called Operation Overlord should be ready by 1 August. The planners were helped by the fact that much work had already been done on similar projects. Combined Operations Headquarters had played a key role in pulling together tri-service experience. The Dieppe raid of August 1942, when a Canadian division had been landed with disastrous results, was amongst the landings from which planners could draw lessons.

RIGHT: US War Bonds poster used in the campaign to raise money to meet the cost of the invasion.

BELOW: After the raid: Dieppe, 19 August 1942, where 2nd Canadian Infantry Division suffered over 3,300 casualties. Fire support was hopelessly inadequate, and planners had not assessed the effect of shingle on tank tracks.

> "I am very uneasy about the whole operation. At the best it will fall so very very far short of the expectations of the bulk of the people, namely those who know nothing of its difficulties. At the worst it may well be the most ghastly disaster of the whole war. I wish to God it were safely over".
>
> Field Marshal Sir Alan Brooke,
> Chief of the Imperial General Staff, 5 June 1944

The Cossac team considered three invasion areas: the Pas de Calais, Normandy and Brittany. The latter was ruled out by distance, both from Britain and from Allied objectives in Europe, and the Pas de Calais was too obvious. It was decided that Normandy, with its large port at Cherbourg, was a better choice. The outline plan envisaged an amphibious assault by three divisions, with airborne divisions dropped on both flanks. There were still unanswered questions, notably who would actually command the invasion, and how enough landing craft could be made available. But in December 1943 it was announced that Eisenhower would take command, with Air Chief Marshal Sir Arthur Tedder as his deputy. All three component commanders were British: General Sir Bernard Montgomery would command ground forces, Admiral Sir Bertram Ramsay naval forces, and Air Chief Marshal Sir Trafford Leigh-Mallory air forces. Montgomery recognized that the blow delivered by the Cossac plan was unlikely to be sufficiently heavy, and in early 1944 he expanded it to comprise an amphibious assault by five divisions with drops by three airborne divisions.

RIGHT: The insignia of the Supreme Head-quarters Allied Expeditionary Forces (SHAEF). The flaming sword represents avenging Allied forces; the black, the darkness of Nazism; and the rainbow, the liberty to come.

NAVAL FORCES ASSIGNED TO OPERATION NEPTUNE (THE NAVAL ASSAULT PHASE)

Naval combatant vessels:	1,213
Landing ships and craft:	4,126
Ancillary ships and craft:	736
Merchant ships:	864
Total:	6,939
British/Canadian:	79%
US:	16.5%
Other allies:	4.5%

133,000 men landed from the sea

OPERATION NEPTUNE 06 JUNE 1944

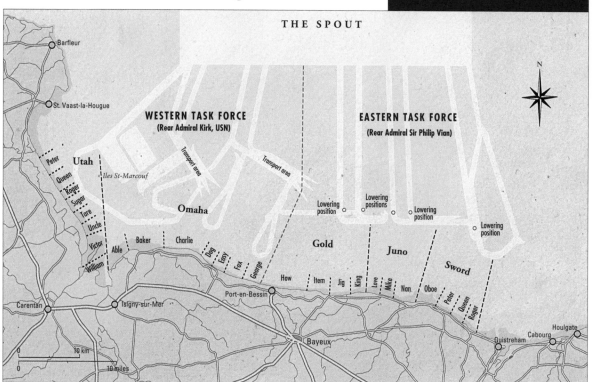

THE SPOUT

Barfleur

St. Vaast-la-Hougue

WESTERN TASK FORCE
(Rear Admiral Kirk, USN)

EASTERN TASK FORCE
(Rear Admiral Sir Philip Vian)

Peter | Utah

Iles St-Marcouf

Queen
Roger
Sugar
Tare
Uncle
Victor
William

Transport area | Transport area

Omaha

Lowering position | Lowering positions | Lowering position | Lowering position

Able | Baker | Charlie | Dog | Easy | Fox | George

Gold | Juno | Sword

How | Item | Jig | King | Love | Mike | Nan | Oboe | Peter | Queen | Roger

Lowering position

Carentan

Isigny-sur-Mer | Port-en-Bessin

Bayeux

Ouistreham | Cabourg | Houlgate

0   10 km
0   10 miles

THE LEADERS

The leaders of the forces that clashed in Normandy presented a sharp contrast.

Although Eisenhower lacked great operational experience, his engaging manner and easy style made him a natural coalition commander.

Tedder had commanded the Mediterranean Allied Air Forces before being appointed Eisenhower's deputy. He was a staunch supporter of Ike's.

Early in 1944 Montgomery was given command of 21st Army Group comprising all Allied land forces committed to D-Day.

Rundstedt, born in 1875, had actually retired in 1938, but commanded army groups in 1940 and 1941. After another spell of retirement he became Commander in Chief West in 1942.

Rommel had an outstanding First World War record as an infantry officer, and was a divisional commander in 1940. He shot to prominence as commander of Axis troops in North Africa.

Dwight Eisenhower, born in 1890, the son of a railway worker, was commissioned in 1913. He saw no action in the First World War, but worked closely with US Army Chief of Staff George C. Marshall and, although decidedly junior, commanded the North African landings in 1942. Eisenhower emerged as a skilful conciliator rather than a flamboyant leader. He had deep reserves of moral courage, and though he can be criticized for spending too long looking up to the military/political level rather than down to the operational/tactical level, his common sense and good nature were invaluable strengths. While Tedder, his British deputy, was devoted to him, the prickly but experienced Montgomery argued that Eisenhower had no real grasp of his task. Ramsay was a hard-working and level-headed naval officer who did much to make Operation Neptune, the naval part of the invasion plan, work well. Leigh-Mallory was an experienced fighter commander, on poor terms with the "bomber barons" whose heavy aircraft froze off the invasion sector. He got on badly with both Coningham, whose Allied Second Tactical Air Force provided air cover in Normandy, and Montgomery, who thought him over-cautious.

The German Commander in Chief West was Field Marshal Gerd von Rundstedt. Born in 1875, Rundstedt served throughout the First World War, retired on age grounds in 1938, but commanded army groups in 1940 and 1941. He was brought back from retirement to be Commander in Chief West in March 1942. Rundstedt was brave, honourable and conventional. He did not enjoy Eisenhower's power, for neither German air nor naval forces in the west (small though both were) answered to him, and his authority was so circumscribed by Hitler that he quipped that the only troops he could move were the sentries at his gates.

Rundstedt clashed with Field Marshal Erwin Rommel, whose Army Group B held the invasion area. Rommel, his reputation made in North Africa, threw his energy into the improvement of beach defences. He argued that the invasion had to be stopped on the beaches, so German armour must be committed early. His experience convinced him that the traditional solution of identifying the main thrust and concentrating to meet it would not work in the face of Allied air power. Hitler imposed a compromise solution which was to leave the armoured divisions of Panzer Group West too far from the coast, and only a single armoured division, 21st Panzer, came into action on D-Day.

The Allies enjoyed advantages before the first shot was fired. Although there was some friction in their chain of command, the structure was logical, and the supreme commander had the temperament for his task. The German system, in contrast, mirrored the conflicting power blocs of the Third Reich, with the heavy hand of Hitler all too apparent.

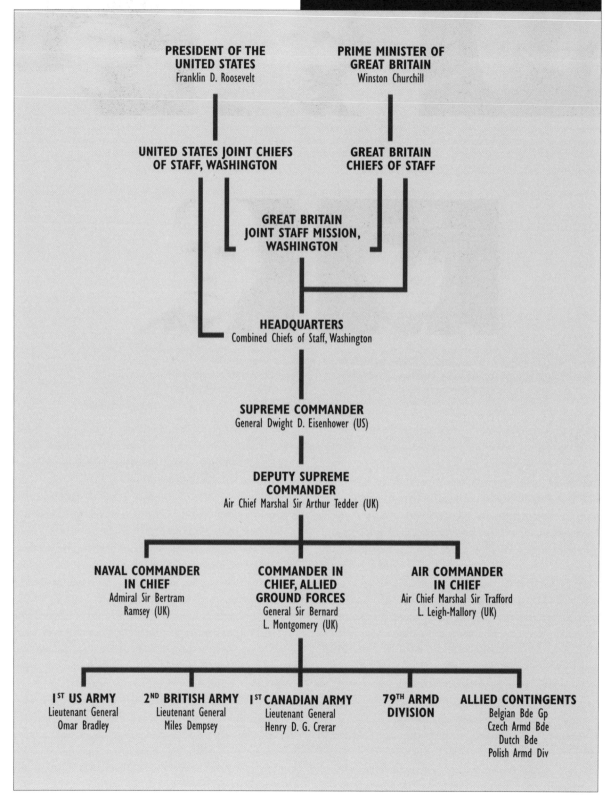

PRESIDENT OF THE UNITED STATES
Franklin D. Roosevelt

PRIME MINISTER OF GREAT BRITAIN
Winston Churchill

UNITED STATES JOINT CHIEFS OF STAFF, WASHINGTON

GREAT BRITAIN CHIEFS OF STAFF

GREAT BRITAIN JOINT STAFF MISSION, WASHINGTON

HEADQUARTERS
Combined Chiefs of Staff, Washington

SUPREME COMMANDER
General Dwight D. Eisenhower (US)

DEPUTY SUPREME COMMANDER
Air Chief Marshal Sir Arthur Tedder (UK)

NAVAL COMMANDER IN CHIEF
Admiral Sir Bertram Ramsey (UK)

COMMANDER IN CHIEF, ALLIED GROUND FORCES
General Sir Bernard L. Montgomery (UK)

AIR COMMANDER IN CHIEF
Air Chief Marshal Sir Trafford L. Leigh-Mallory (UK)

1ST US ARMY
Lieutenant General Omar Bradley

2ND BRITISH ARMY
Lieutenant General Miles Dempsey

1ST CANADIAN ARMY
Lieutenant General Henry D. G. Crerar

79TH ARMD DIVISION

ALLIED CONTINGENTS
Belgian Bde Gp
Czech Armd Bde
Dutch Bde
Polish Armd Div

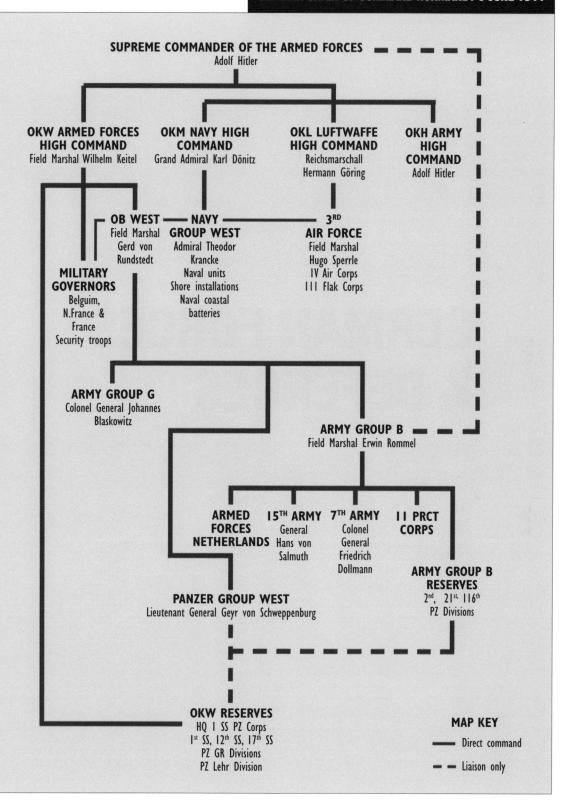

GERMAN CHAIN OF COMMAND NORMANDY 6 JUNE 1944

SUPREME COMMANDER OF THE ARMED FORCES
Adolf Hitler

OKW ARMED FORCES HIGH COMMAND
Field Marshal Wilhelm Keitel

OKM NAVY HIGH COMMAND
Grand Admiral Karl Dönitz

OKL LUFTWAFFE HIGH COMMAND
Reichsmarschall Hermann Göring

OKH ARMY HIGH COMMAND
Adolf Hitler

OB WEST
Field Marshal Gerd von Rundstedt

NAVY GROUP WEST
Admiral Theodor Krancke
Naval units
Shore installations
Naval coastal batteries

3RD AIR FORCE
Field Marshal Hugo Sperrle
IV Air Corps
III Flak Corps

MILITARY GOVERNORS
Belguim,
N.France &
France
Security troops

ARMY GROUP G
Colonel General Johannes Blaskowitz

ARMY GROUP B
Field Marshal Erwin Rommel

ARMED FORCES NETHERLANDS

15TH ARMY
General Hans von Salmuth

7TH ARMY
Colonel General Friedrich Dollmann

II PRCT CORPS

ARMY GROUP B RESERVES
2nd, 21st, 116th
PZ Divisions

PANZER GROUP WEST
Lieutenant General Geyr von Schweppenburg

OKW RESERVES
HQ I SS PZ Corps
1st SS, 12th SS, 17th SS
PZ GR Divisions
PZ Lehr Division

MAP KEY
—— Direct command
- - - Liaison only

GERMAN FORCES & DEFENCES

For the Germans, the west was "a poor man's war" overshadowed by the struggle against the Russians.

Rundstedt was responsible for the whole of France and the Low Countries, with 1st and 19th Armies of Army Group G covering the area south of the Loire, 7th and 15th Armies of Army Group B dealing with the Loire to the Dutch border, and Armed Forces Netherlands holding Holland. He had to do much with little. General Blumentritt, his chief of staff, complained that there was insufficient motor transport: infantry divisions had to rely on horses. Air attacks had reduced the flow of fuel, ammunition and spares, and many units had to detrain so far back that they were already tired by the time they came into battle. Some formations, like the SS Panzer divisions, were very good indeed, but others had been worn down by combat in the east and had not yet been fully reconstituted. Coastal divisions had weak artillery and little inherent mobility. Many of their officers and men had already been wounded, and one division was composed entirely of men with stomach ailments. The Germans made wide use of *Osttruppen*, recruited from amongst Russian prisoners of war and comprising a variety of national and ethnic groups: there were no less than 21 "Russian" battalions in the 7th Army alone. Blumentritt identified 25 different types of division which varied in composition, with requirements for spares and ammunition which made them a quartermaster's nightmare.

PREVIOUS PAGE: An aerial photograph, taken just before D-Day, shows a variety of beach defences exposed at low water: most were designed to disable landing craft.

BELOW: This propaganda shot shows a fast-firing MG 34 machine gun in a beach bunker. The soldier on the right has two stick grenades to hand.

FRIEDRICH DOLLMANN

Dollman was commissioned into the Bavarian field artillery in 1901 and spent the First World War in regimental and staff appointments. He commanded 7th Army in the 1940 campaign, earning the Knight's Cross and promotion to colonel general. Dollmann remained in the same post, and by 1944 lacked any recent combat experience. Criticized by Hitler for permitting the fall of Cherbourg, Dollmann probably committed suicide at Le Mans on 28 June, though formal records attribute his death to a heart attack.

GERMAN ANTI-TANK OBSTACLES USED AS UNDERWATER OBSTACLES

TETRAHEDRA.I.

2'6 or 4.0 high.

TETRAHEDRA. II

2'6 or 4.0 high

GERMAN STEEL OBSTACLES—HEDGEHOG

5'7"

N.B. Has also been seen supported on stakes, making overall effective height of 8ft.

Page N° A

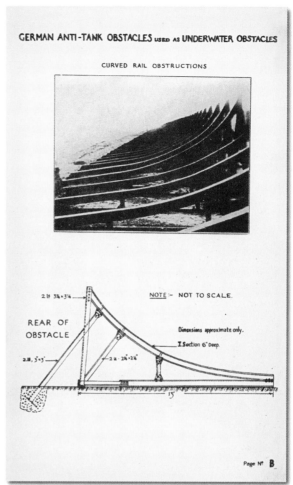

GERMAN ANTI-TANK OBSTACLES USED AS UNDERWATER OBSTACLES

CURVED RAIL OBSTRUCTIONS

REAR OF OBSTACLE

NOTE :- NOT TO SCALE.

Dimensions approximate only.

I Section 6" Deep.

Page N° B

ABOVE: Top-secret Allied documents showing details of German beach defences.

RIGHT: A 1943 German photograph shows the erection of beach defences. These anti-landing obstacles were primitive by the standards of the Atlantic Wall in June 1944.

Although the Germans were certain that the Allies would indeed invade – in November 1943 Hitler issued a directive foreseeing an offensive "not later than the spring, perhaps earlier" – they were unsure as to time and place. Most generals, deciding on the basis of traditional military education, thought the Pas de Calais, the most direct route, a more likely objective than Normandy. Hitler, reasoning intuitively, suspected that Normandy was more probable, but General Walter Warlimont admitted that his comrades were "not quite convinced" by this. The Germans were in a state of acute air inferiority, although many generals argued that this had less effect on the outcome of individual battles than it did on movement behind the lines. "It was like pitting a racehorse against a motor car," wrote one.

Yet it was not that simple. The Germans had some first-rate weapons, like the 88mm anti-tank gun, and tanks like the Panther and Tiger. Until defeats in the east and west in mid-1944 struck fatal damage to its replacement system, the German army took more time and trouble to train senior NCOs than the British and Americans took to train junior officers. And if the fighting on the Eastern Front had done terrible damage to the Germans, it had also left them with a hard-forged nucleus of experienced junior commanders, men like Michael Wittmann, who almost single-handedly stopped the British 7th Armoured Division on 14 June, and Hans von Luck, whose determination did so much to thwart British plans in Operation Goodwood the following month. Allied policy of offering Germany only unconditional surrender persuaded many German soldiers, even if they had little sympathy with the Nazis, that failure in Normandy would result in the invasion of their homeland. The defenders of Normandy were certainly not supermen: but this was an army with proud traditions, fighting with its back to the wall against adversaries who enjoyed quantitative superiority but often lacked experience and the sheer killer instinct.

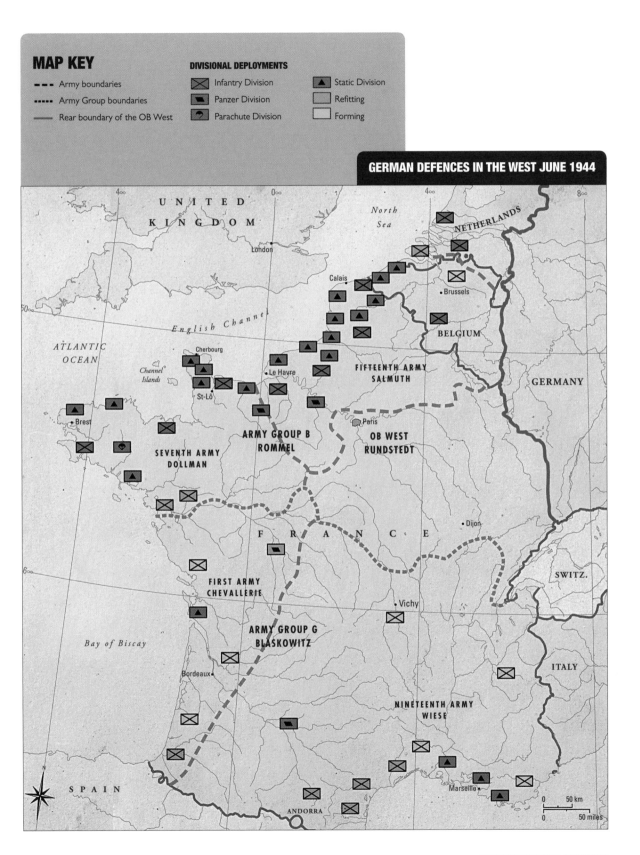

MAP KEY

--- Army boundaries

···· Army Group boundaries

— Rear boundary of the OB West

DIVISIONAL DEPLOYMENTS

Infantry Division

Panzer Division

Parachute Division

Static Division

Refitting

Forming

GERMAN DEFENCES IN THE WEST JUNE 1944

UNITED KINGDOM

London

North Sea

NETHERLANDS

ATLANTIC OCEAN

English Channel

Calais

Brussels

BELGIUM

GERMANY

Channel Islands

Cherbourg

Le Havre

St-Lô

FIFTEENTH ARMY
SALMUTH

Brest

ARMY GROUP B
ROMMEL

Paris

OB WEST
RUNDSTEDT

SEVENTH ARMY
DOLLMAN

Dijon

SWITZ.

F R A N C E

FIRST ARMY
CHEVALLERIE

Bay of Biscay

Vichy

Bordeaux

ARMY GROUP G
BLASKOWITZ

ITALY

NINETEENTH ARMY
WIESE

SPAIN

Marseille

ANDORRA

0   50 km

0   50 miles

DECEPTION & INTELLIGENCE

If the Germans had obtained timely and accurate information, they could have stopped the invasion in its tracks: intelligence and deception were fundamental to the campaign's outcome.

The Allies had to glean information on a wide range of factors, to keep their own preparations secret and to persuade the Germans that the invasion would take place elsewhere.

The British had penetrated German ciphers to produce invaluable signals intelligence known as Ultra (short for Top Secret Ultra). They had also cracked the Japanese diplomatic cipher, so that reports sent from Berlin to Tokyo fell into their hands. And while German agents in Britain had fared badly, the double agent Garbo (a Spaniard called Juan Pujol) fed the Germans a rich diet of misinformation, helping convince them that the Normandy landings were one part of a two-pronged thrust, with the second aimed at the Pas de Calais.

Operation Fortitude relayed the same message on a larger scale. A fictitious First US Army Group (FUSAG) was "stationed" in south-east England, and fake camps and spurious radio traffic were designed to persuade the Germans that substantial forces were ready for the short hop across the Channel. Fortitude North produced a fictitious 4th Army in Scotland, ready to invade Norway. German intelligence, like the chain of command in Normandy, lacked a single controlling voice, and its various agencies "vied with each other in supplying Hitler with reports".

Allied intelligence on Normandy came from many sources. The BBC appealed for holiday postcards of the whole of France, and relevant ones were collated. The French Resistance produced information on German defences and deployments. Some air photographs revealed the landscape from above, while others, taken from low-flying aircraft, helped create the beach panorama

ABOVE: The 25-pound field gun was the workhorse of British artillery. This dummy gun, limber and truck, intended to deceive an observer from 500 to 1,000 yards, were collapsible and folded flat for stowage.

PREVIOUS PAGE: These full-sized dummy Landing Craft, Tanks (LCT), each 160 feet long, were used in harbours in south-east England to suggest that the invasion would be directed at the Pas de Calais.

which would be visible from landing craft. Although the Allied air forces softened up objectives in Normandy, more bombs were dropped outside the invasion sector than within it. Experts made night-time landings on Normandy beaches to take sand samples which would help ascertain their load-bearing capacity. By the time D-Day arrived the Allies enjoyed excellent intelligence, while their opponents were shrouded by the fog of war.

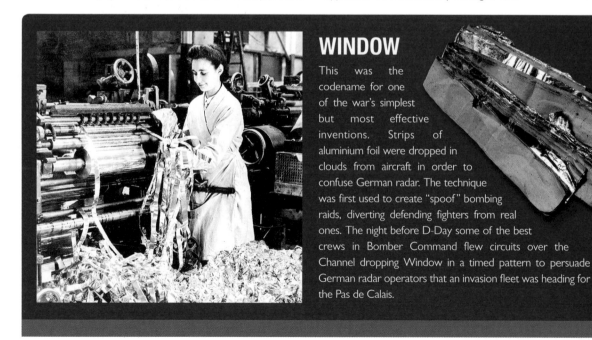

WINDOW

This was the codename for one of the war's simplest but most effective inventions. Strips of aluminium foil were dropped in clouds from aircraft in order to confuse German radar. The technique was first used to create "spoof" bombing raids, diverting defending fighters from real ones. The night before D-Day some of the best crews in Bomber Command flew circuits over the Channel dropping Window in a timed pattern to persuade German radar operators that an invasion fleet was heading for the Pas de Calais.

"Genfldm von Runsdtedt and his staff expected the invasion ... somewhere between Calais and the mouth of the Seine. This was the most vulnerable area for the shortest thrust through northern France and Belgium into germany and the ruhr."

General Gunther Blumentritt, Chief of Staff, Commander in Chief West

ABOVE: This pneumatic dummy Sherman tank, made by Dunlop Rubber Company, could be blown up like a balloon.

RIGHT: When deflated, the dummy Sherman tank fitted into a valise only slightly larger than a sports bag.

THE RESISTANCE
& SOE

German victory in 1940 divided France. There were those who agreed with Marshal Pétain, head of the new French state based at the spa town of Vichy, that defeat was the outcome of decadence. And there were others who believed in armed resistance.

There were some stirrings early on, and the German invasion of Russia in 1941 brought French Communists into the struggle. However, the Resistance grew gradually, and was marked by the factionalism which mirrored French politics.

In 1940 the Special Operations Executive (SOE) was set up "to co-ordinate all action, by way of subversion and sabotage, against the enemy overseas...." It was divided into "country sections", though France was the responsibility of several sections. Section RF worked with General de Gaulle's Free French in London, but Section F did not, and SOE's historian observes that inter-section jealousies "often raged with virulence". The US equivalent of SOE, the Office of Strategic Services (OSS), also maintained a French section.

SOE recruited men and women from a cross-section of British and French society. A young peer was killed in Normandy in 1942; a successful sabotage team was led by a fireman and a garage hand. Agents were sent to France by parachute or Westland Lysander light aircraft. They carried out numerous tasks, from sabotage of key installations, through the collection of intelligence to the organization of arms drops. If captured they could expect no mercy. As their historian wrote: "The best died silent; or if they had to talk, said nothing the enemy wanted to hear."

PREVIOUS PAGE: In an image replete with symbolism, local people inspect a multi-barrelled Nebelwerfer (Moaning Minnie to Allied soldiers) captured at Fleury-sur-Orne. The bunker behind sheltered villagers during the subsequent fighting.

BELOW: *Crève-pneus* – a box of mines used by the French Resistance for blowing up the tyres of German vehicles. No identifying marks of any kind were used on equipment dropped by the Allies for use by the Resistance.

LEFT: Resistance groups used weapons parachuted in by the Allies or captured from the Germans. This truck bears the Cross of Lorraine, and FFI for Forces Françaises de l'Intérieur.

RIGHT: Assignment orders for Operation Hardtack 24, which were given to Free French Commandos in January 1944 for their reconnaissance of the invasion area at Utah Beach.

SECRET

INTELLIGENCE REQUIREMENTS

OPERATION HARDTACK 24

TOPOGRAPHICAL.

Beach

1. Describe nature and firmness of beach where crossed.

2. Recover samples of sand from below and above high water mark.

3. Describe nature and dimensions of runnels on beach.

Wall.

4. Nature and dimensions of wall or bank between high water mark and dunes - is it an obstacle to infantry, MT and/or AFVs?

Dunes.

5. How easy is movement through the dunes for infantry, MT and/or AFVs?

6. How easy is it to recognise a given spot or skyline in the dunes from seaward?

7. How good is cover for infantry in the dunes?

Floods.

8. Limits of any flooded area met?

9. Exact depth of flooding (state places of measurement)?

10. Extent to which flooded or saturated ground forms obstacle to movement.

11. Are roads and tracks across flooding clear of water? If so how high, and by how wide and firm a verge?

12. Recover sample of mud from below flood water.

Roads.

13. What are dimensions and conditions of all roads and tracks? Are there any signs of prepared road or bridge demolitions?

DEFENCES.

14. Detailed description with measurements of any underwater obstacles, including details of apparent condition and method of fixing into ground.

15. Details of any wire fences encountered (size, layout, type and fixing of pickets); recovery of specimen wire strands and of any attached warning devices.

16. Details of any minefields encountered, giving:-

> Type of mine
> spacing
> use of tripwires
> marking and fencing-off.

56 484

Recovery of a specimen mine would be useful but is not essential.

Resistance groups made a major contribution to the Allied war effort in 1944, by providing intelligence on defences (one bicycle-racer from Bayeux regularly sped along the coast road with plans concealed in his handle-bars) and by the methodical sabotage of rail and telephone communications. In March 1944 de Gaulle decreed that the Resistance would be assimilated into the French army as the Forces Françaises de l'Intérieur, but Communist FTP groups generally declined to obey. Although the importance of the Resistance was later exaggerated, it was important both for its practical work and for the way it kept the soul of France alive.

RIGHT: Railway-track bomb detonator used by the French Resistance in Normandy. Disruption of the railway network played an important part in reducing the flow of German reinforcements to the invasion area.

FAR RIGHT: Heavy bombers of the US 8th Air Force, based in Britain, dropping weapons and equipment to the Resistance in 1944.

BELOW: The Resistance made a valuable contribution to the "War of the Rails". This railway depot on the German lines of communication was sabotaged in March 1944.

VIOLETTE SZABO

Szabo was the spirited daughter of an English father and French mother who married a Free French officer in 1940. She joined SOE in 1943, and was parachuted into France on a reconnaissance mission in April 1944. Recovered by a Lysander light aircraft, she was parachuted into Limoges 24 hours after D-Day to help co-ordinate Resistance work with the Allied invasion. However, she encountered a German patrol and was captured when her ammunition ran out. Subsequently shot in Ravensbruck concentration camp, she was awarded a posthumous George Cross, Britain's supreme award for gallantry off the field of battle.

Le général Eisenhower s'adresse aux peuples des Pays Occupés

PEUPLES DE L'EUROPE OCCIDENTALE:

Les troupes des Forces Expéditionnaires Alliées ont débarqué sur les côtes de France.

Ce débarquement fait partie du plan concerté par les Nations Unies, conjointement avec nos grands alliés Russes, pour la libération de l'Europe.

C'est à vous tous que j'adresse ce message. Même si le premier assaut n'a pas eu lieu sur votre territoire, l'heure de votre libération approche.

Tous les patriotes, hommes ou femmes, jeunes ou vieux, ont un rôle à jouer dans notre marche vers la victoire finale. Aux membres des mouvements de Résistance dirigés de l'intérieur ou de l'extérieur, je dis : "Suivez les instructions que vous avez reçues !" Aux patriotes qui ne sont point membres de groupes de Résistance organisés, je dis : "Continuez votre résistance auxiliaire, mais n'exposez pas vos vies inutilement ; attendez l'heure où je vous donnerai le signal de vous dresser et de frapper l'ennemi. Le jour viendra où j'aurai besoin de votre force unie." Jusqu'à ce jour, je compte sur vous pour vous plier à la dure obligation d'une discipline impassible.

CITOYENS FRANÇAIS:

Je suis fier de commander une fois de plus les vaillants soldats de France. Luttant côte à côte avec leurs Alliées, ils s'apprêtent à prendre leur pleine part dans la libération de leur Patrie natale.

Parce que le premier débarquement a eu lieu sur votre territoire, je répète pour vous, avec une insistance encore plus grande, mon message aux peuples des autres pays occupés de l'Europe Occidentale. Suivez les instructions de vos chefs. Un soulèvement prématuré de tous les Français risque de vous empêcher, quand l'heure décisive aura sonné, de mieux servir encore votre pays. Ne vous énervez pas, et restez en alerte !

Comme Commandant Suprême des Forces Expéditionnaires Alliées, j'ai le devoir et la responsabilité de prendre toutes les mesures nécessaires à la conduite de la guerre. Je sais que je puis compter sur vous pour obeir aux ordres que je serai appelé à promulguer.

L'administration civile de la France doit effectivement être assurée, par des Français. Chacun doit demeurer à son poste, à moins qu'il ne reçoive des instructions contraires. Ceux qui ont fait cause commune avec l'ennemi, et qui ont ainsi trahi leur patrie, seront révoqués. Quand la France sera libérée de ses oppresseurs, vous choisirez vous-mêmes vos représentants ainsi que le Gouvernement sous l'autorité duquel vous voudrez vivre.

Au cours de cette campagne qui a pour but l'écrasement définitif de l'ennemi, peut-être aurez-vous à subir encore des pertes et des destructions. Mais, si tragiques que soient ces épreuves, elles font partie du prix qu'exige la victoire. Je vous garantis que je ferai tout en mon pouvoir pour atténuer vos épreuves. Je sais que je puis compter sur votre fermeté, qui n'est pas moins grande aujourd'hui que par le passé. Les héroïques exploits des Français qui ont continué la lutte contre les Nazis et contre leurs satellites de Vichy, en France, en Italie et dans l'Empire français, ont été pour nous tous un modèle et une inspiration.

Ce débarquement ne fait que commencer la campagne d'Europe Occidentale. Nous sommes à la veille de grandes batailles. Je demande à tous les hommes qui aiment la liberté d'être des nôtres. Que rien n'ébranle votre foi — rien non plus n'arrêtera nos coups — ENSEMBLE, NOUS VAINCRONS.

Dwight D Eisenhower

DWIGHT D. EISENHOWER,
Commandant Suprême des
Forces Expéditionnaires Alliées

Z.F.1.

LEFT AND BELOW: Aerial leaflet containing a message about the invasion, addressed to the citizens of Occupied Europe from Supreme Allied Commander General Dwight D. Eisenhower, copies of which were dropped by Allied aircraft on the French population in Normandy.

LES ARMEES ALLIEES DEBARQUENT

PEGASUS BRIDGE

The bridges over the Caen Canal and the River Orne – the former codenamed Pegasus and the latter Horsa – provided a crucial link between invasion beaches and airborne landings. In British hands, they would enable armour landed by sea to operate east of the river.

Held by the Germans, they might form a barrier between sea-landed and airborne forces, or enable German tanks to take the landings in the flank.

They would be seized by glider assault by Major John Howard's D Company, 2nd Battalion, The Oxfordshire and Buckinghamshire Light Infantry. Howard had been a regular army NCO before the war, and was an Oxford policeman in 1939. Having rejoined the army, he was commissioned in 1940. He commanded a tough company, and placed special emphasis on night training. Howard had three platoons, and was reinforced by two more, and a troop of engineers. The force would land in six Horsa gliders, three for each bridge, with Howard leading the assault on Pegasus and Captain Brian Priday that on Horsa. The company had a close relationship with its pilots. When aerial photographs revealed that the Germans were digging holes for anti-glider poles, Staff Sergeant Jim Wallwork, Howard's pilot, told the men that even if the poles were in place they would help by slowing down the overloaded gliders.

PREVIOUS PAGE: Allied troops in control of Pegasus Bridge. John Howard's Glider Number 1 is still visible across the canal.

RIGHT: The Colt .45 pistol carried by Captain Vaughan of the Royal Army Medical Corps, who was in Glider 3 of Major John Howard's assault force at Pegasus Bridge.

BELOW: Gliders Numbers 1 and 2 within yards of Pegasus Bridge. Behind the line of trees the Café Gondrée, the first French building to be liberated on D-Day, is visible across the Caen Canal.

JOHN HOWARD

Howard had left the regular army before the war, joining the Oxford police in 1939. Recalled to service, he rose rapidly and received a commission in 1940. His company was specially selected for its D-Day mission, and he was awarded the Distinguished Service Order for his achievement. Slightly wounded, he was more seriously hit later, and was badly injured in a jeep crash that November. A civil servant after the war, he remained a respected figure on veterans' visits to Normandy.

5 Par Bde OO no. 1 Apex A.

Ref Maps.   1/50,000 Sheets 7/F1, 7/F2
            1/25,000 Sheet No. 40/16 NW.

To: Maj RJ HOWARD, 2 OXF BUCKS.

INFM

1. Enemy

   (a) Static def in area of ops.

   Garrison of the two brs at BENOUVILLE 098748 and RANVILLE 104746 consists
   of about 50 men, armed with four LAA guns, probably 20 mm, four to six IMG,
   one AA MG and possibly two A Tk guns of less than 50cm cal. A concrete
   shelter is under constr, and the br will have been prepared for demolition.
   See ph enlargement A21.

   (b) Mobile res in area of ops.

   One bn of 736 GR is in the area LEBISEY 0471 - BIEVILLE 0674 with probably 8
   to 12 tks under comd. This bn is either wholly or partially carried in MT
   and will have at least one coy standing by as an anti-airtps picket.

   Bn HQ of the RIGHT coastal bn of 736 GR is in the area 065772. At least one
   pl will be available in this area as a fighting patrol, ready to move out at
   once to seek infm.

   (c) State of Alertness.

   The large scale preparations necessary for the invasion of the Continent, the
   suitability of moon and tide will combine to produce a high state of alertness
   in the GERMAN def. The br grn may be standing to, and charges will have been
   laid in the demolition chambers.

   (d) Detailed infm on enemy def and res is available on demand from Div Int
        Summaries, air phs and models.

2. OWN Tps.

   (a) 5 Para Bde drops immediately NE of RANVILLE at H minus 4 hrs 30 mins, and
        moves forthwith to take up a def posn round the two brs.

   (b) 3 Para Bde drops at H minus 4 hrs 30 mins and is denying to the enemy the
        high wooded ground SOUTH of LE MESNIL 1472.

   (c) 6 Airldg Bde is ldg NE of RANVILLE and WEST of BENOUVILLE at about H plus
        12 hrs, and moves thence to a def posn in the area STE HONORINE LA
        CHARDONNERETTE 0971 - ESCOVILLE 1271.

   (d) 3 Br Div is ldg WEST of OUISTREHAM 1079 at H hr with objective CAEN.

3. Ground.

   See available maps, air ph and models.

INTENTION

4. Your task is to seize intact the Brs over R.Orne and canal at BENOUVILLE
    098748 and RANVILLE 104746, and to hold them until relief by 7 Para Bn. If
    the brs are blown, you will est personnel ferries over both water obstacles
    as soon as possible.

METHOD.

5. Composition of force

LEFT: The orders received by Major John Howard for the assault on Pegasus Ridge.

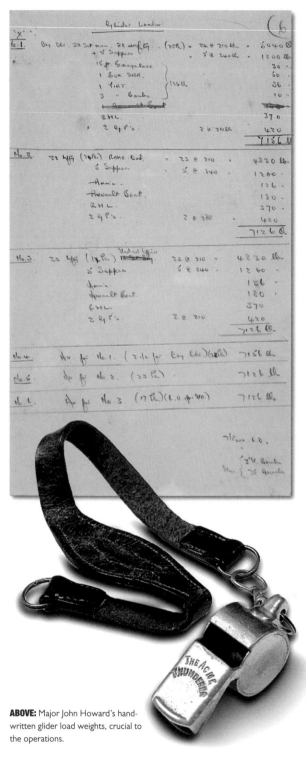

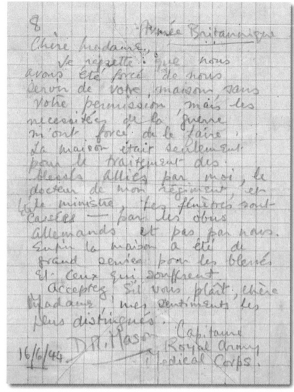

ABOVE: Letter written in perfect French by Captain Mason of the Royal Army Medical Corps to the absent owner of a house in the British 6th Airborne Division's zone of control. He apologizes for using the house without permission, and points out that the broken windows were caused by the German shells and not by the British medics.

LEFT: British 6th Airborne Division.

ABOVE: Major John Howard's hand-written glider load weights, crucial to the operations.

ABOVE RIGHT: Major Howard's "Acme Thunderer" whistle, worn round his neck during the assault on Pegasus Bridge, and used to rally his troops in the dark.

Wallwork took off from Tarrant Rushton at 10.56 pm on 5 June, and landed near the eastern end of Pegasus just after midnight. One man was killed in the landing, but within minutes Howard's team had secured the bridge, only Lieutenant Den Brotheridge being killed. Although the troops attacking Horsa landed further from it, their assault was also successful, and Howard ordered his radio operator to send the success signal, "Ham and Jam". There were sporadic German probes during the night and the following morning, but not the armoured counter-attack that the British feared. Howard's men were reinforced by paras during the night and at about 1.00 pm on 6 June they heard bagpipes heralding the approach of Lord Lovat's 1st Special Services Brigade from the beaches. They had taken the bridges as ordered, and held them till relieved.

MACHINE GUN
EMPLACEMENT
× × ×
× × ×
BARBED
WIRE
× × ×
PILLBOX
(LATER HOWARD'S H.Q.) ×

× × ×
×

ANTI-TANK
GUN

HORSA BRIDGE →

CANAL DE CAEN

N

TRENCHES
AND
BUNKERS

1

PEGASUS BRIDGE

GLIDERS

2

3

HORSA BRIDGE

BELOW: Aerial reconnaissance photograph showing Pegasus Bridge over the Caen Canal and Horsa Bridge over the Orne River after Major Howard's attack.

LEFT: Aerial reconnaissance photograph showing the three Horsa gliders of Major John Howard's Pegasus Bridge assault force. Note the broken fuselage of Glider Number 2, caused by pilot Oliver Boland's last-minute swerve to avoid hitting the lead glider.

BRITISH AIRBORNE ASSAULT

The British 6th Airborne Division, commanded by Major General Richard "Windy" Gale, was dropped between the River Orne and the high ground of the Bois de Bavent to secure the eastern flank of the invasion sector.

Some of its units had special missions: a reinforced glider company, as we have seen, seized Pegasus Bridge. The 9th Parachute Battalion was to take the German coastal battery at Merville. Its plan was disrupted when some attackers were dropped far away, and although the guns (which proved to be smaller-calibre than had been expected) were put out of action, the battery was briefly reoccupied by the Germans. Men of 3rd Parachute Squadron Royal Engineers were to destroy the bridges over the River Bures so as to prevent the Germans using them. They succeeded in destroying those at Troarn, Bures and Robehomme, and with the assistance of 1st Canadian Parachute Battalion, that over a tributary stream at Varaville.

The division's two parachute brigades, 3rd and 5th, were dropped during the night, and most units were widely scattered. Many soldiers spent a confusing night endeavouring to link up with their comrades in the darkness, colliding with German patrols and securing strongpoints. One estimate suggests that not more than 60 per cent of the 4,800 men of the division who were landed in France on D-Day were actually able to participate in the day's fighting. On the morning of 6 June, 4th Airlanding Brigade began to arrive by glider, and with it came heavy engineer stores, light tanks and jeeps, field and anti-tank guns, putting the division in a much better position to resist any attack by German armour. It is a measure of the risks run by glider pilots that 71 of the 196 who landed became casualties.

ABOVE: This photograph, taken on 5 June, shows Horsa gliders on the runway with the Halifax bombers that will tow them to France standing ready. All aircraft bear the Allied recognition stripes.

BELOW: Shoulder patch and "wings" worn by British glider pilots.

BRITISH AIRBORNE ASSAULT

RIGHT: The main airborne drop was preceded by the arrival of Pathfinders who set up beacons to mark dropping zones. These Path-finders are synchronizing their watches before boarding their aircraft.

BELOW: Two military police NCOs of 6th Airborne Division guard a crossroads near the village of Ranville on 9 July. There is a Horsa glider in the background.

Although the eastern flank was now largely secure, it was certainly anything but quiet. The village of Bréville, up on the ridge overlooking the main glider landing zone, was the one hole in the division's perimeter. On the night of 12 June it was attacked by a scratch force based on the much-depleted 12th Parachute Battalion. The two brigadiers involved were wounded, and 12th Parachute Battalion lost 141 of the 160 officers and men who attacked, including the commanding officer. However, by dawn the village was secured, and Major General Gale later declared that its seizure was the turning point in the fight for the Orne bridgehead. It is axiomatic that airborne troops are best used for operations requiring dash, and should be withdrawn as soon as their objectives have been taken. But 6th Airborne Division remained up on the hard shoulder it had created throughout the long and bloody Normandy summer, demonstrating that it could cope with a long attritional slog as well as with the dangerous chaos of an airborne assault.

RICHARD "WINDY" GALE

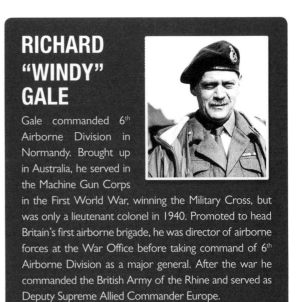

Gale commanded 6th Airborne Division in Normandy. Brought up in Australia, he served in the Machine Gun Corps in the First World War, winning the Military Cross, but was only a lieutenant colonel in 1940. Promoted to head Britain's first airborne brigade, he was director of airborne forces at the War Office before taking command of 6th Airborne Division as a major general. After the war he commanded the British Army of the Rhine and served as Deputy Supreme Allied Commander Europe.

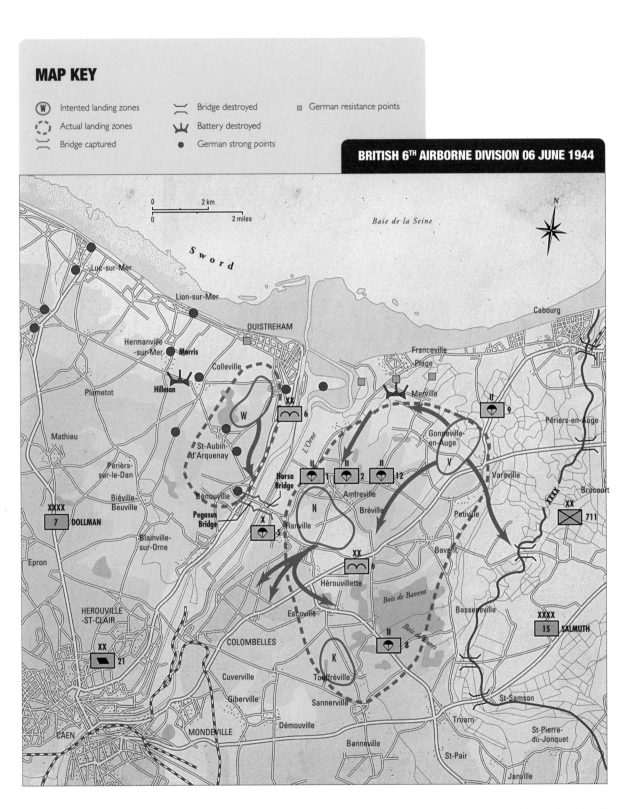

MAP KEY

(W) Intented landing zones

⌣⌣ Bridge destroyed

▢ German resistance points

(◌) Actual landing zones

Ẅ Battery destroyed

(:): Bridge captured

● German strong points

BRITISH 6ᵀᴴ AIRBORNE DIVISION 06 JUNE 1944

0 — 2 km
0 — 2 miles

Baie de la Seine

N

Luc-sur-Mer

Lion-sur-Mer

Cabourg

S w o r d

OUISTREHAM

Hermanville
-sur-Mer **Morris**

Franceville
Plage

Colleville

Hillman

Merville

II 9

Plumetot

W

XX 6

Périers-en-Auge

Mathieu

St-Aubin-
d'Arquenay

L'Orne

Gonneville-
en-Auge

Périers-
sur-le-Dan

II 1

II 2

II 12

V

Varaville

Brucourt

Biéville-
Beuville

**Horsa
Bridge**

Amfreville

XXXX
7 **DOLLMAN**

**Pegasus
Bridge**

Bénouville

Bréville

XXXX
XX 711

Petiville

Blainville-
sur-Orne

X 5

Ranville

N

Epron

XX 6

Bavent

HEROUVILLE
-ST-CLAIR

Hérouvillette

Bois de Bavent

Basseville

XX 21

Escoville

COLOMBELLES

K

II 8

Bois de Bures

XXXX
15 **SALMUTH**

Cuverville

Touffréville

St-Samson

Giberville

Sannerville

CAEN

MONDEVILLE

Démouville

Banneville

Troarn

St-Pierre-
du-Jonquet

St-Pair

Janville

BRITISH AIRBORNE ASSAULT

US AIRBORNE ASSAULT

Two US airborne divisions, Major General Matthew B. Ridgway's 82nd and Major General Maxwell Taylor's 101st, were to land at the base of the Cotentin peninsula on the western flank of the invasion beaches.

Each had two three-battalion parachute infantry regiments and one glider infantry regiment, with supporting artillery and engineers. Some planners favoured a bolder project, the establishment of an airhead in the area of Evreux and Dreux to threaten the Seine crossings and Paris, but Eisenhower, arguing that the force would be vulnerable once it had landed, favoured a more conservative option. However, some argued that the Cotentin plan was risky enough as it stood. Leigh-Mallory called it "a very speculative operation", and had it modified so that many of the gliders would arrive on the evening of D-Day.

It was eventually decided that 101st Airborne Division would be dropped behind Utah Beach, to secure the beach exits and be

ABOVE: A stick of parachutists ready to jump above the Cotentin early on 6 June. The heavily laden men have hooked their static lines, which will open their chutes, onto the cable above them.

LEFT: US 101st Airbourne Division.

MAXWELL D. TAYLOR

Taylor was commissioned from West Point in 1922 but was only a major when war broke out. Quickly promoted, he commanded the artillery of 82nd Airborne Division, and in 1943 carried out a dangerous mission behind the lines in Italy. He led 101st Airborne Division in Normandy and in Operation Market Garden in September. He later served as Chief of Staff of the US Army, Chairman of the Joint Chiefs, and US Ambassador to Vietnam.

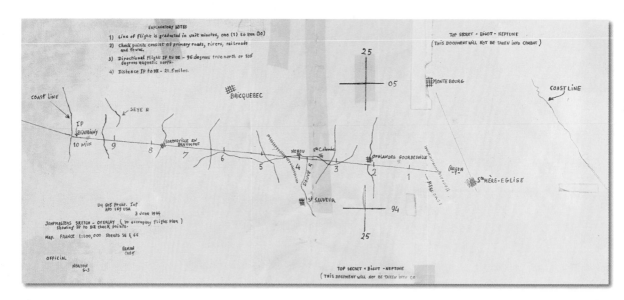

prepared to exploit through Carentan. 82nd Airborne Division was to land further north-west, astride the River Merderet, to capture the crossings over the river, seize the little town of Ste-Mère-Eglise, on the main Cherbourg-Bayeux road, and be prepared to exploit westwards. The Germans had flooded the valleys, turning the area into a patchwork of inundated fields laced with deeper watercourses and dotted with solidly built Norman villages and farms.

The first wave of parachutists, some 13,000 men, was to be dropped from 822 C-47 aircraft. Many pilots lacked experience for their demanding task, and in the early hours of 6 June this became even more difficult as a bank of thick cloud confronted them as they flew in from the east. A mixture of poor visibility and ground fire scattered the aircraft and, with them, the parachutists they dropped. Some were released too late and fell into the sea, or drowned in flooded rivers: others hit trees or roofs. Most who landed safely were hopelessly lost, and spent the night searching

ABOVE: Top-secret hand-drawn map showing the minute-by-minute position on the way in to the drop zone just west of Ste-Mere-Eglise for elements of the 505th Parachute Infantry Regiment of the 82nd Airborne Division.

RIGHT: One of the "crickets" carried by US airborne troops on their D-Day jump. They were used to distinguish friend from foe in the dark: one click was to be answered by two.

for other Americans, bumping into German patrols, with losses on both sides, or simply sleeping.

Much of 505th Parachute Infantry Regiment of 82nd Airborne Division was dropped close to Ste-Mère-Eglise: one soldier landed with his parachute hooked onto the town church's steeple and survived, but others were less lucky, and fell among the garrison, alerted by Allied bombing of the village. The place was secured early on, and the vital road was blocked after a spirited action at Neuville. By the end of the day, 82nd Airborne was strongly

MATTHEW B. RIDGWAY

Ridgway joined the infantry from West Point in 1917. In 1939 he accompanied US Army Chief of Staff George C. Marshall on a mission to South America. Ridgway commanded 82nd Infantry Division in 1942, supervising its conversion to an airborne formation. After leading his division in Normandy he commanded XVIII Airborne Corps. In 1950 he succeeded Douglas MacArthur at the head of the US Eighth Army in Korea, and was US Army Chief of Staff 1953–56.

posted around Ste-Mère-Eglise, but was in contact neither with the troops coming ashore at Utah Beach nor with the 101st. It had lost over 1,200 men, over half of them missing. Maxwell Taylor's men were more fortunate. Although only about 2,500 of the 6,600 men dropped had assembled by the evening of D-Day, they seized many of their objectives, and secured the exits from Utah Beach and some of the bridges near Carentan.

The inaccuracy of the drops helped to confuse the Germans, whose senior commanders spent the early hours of 6 June confronted by reports which gave no clear pointer to Allied intentions. Many were away at a war game at Rennes, and one divisional commander, Lieutenant General Wilhelm Falley, was killed when he encountered a party of parachutists. Like the British drop, the American airborne assault did not go according to plan, but it too fulfilled its task.

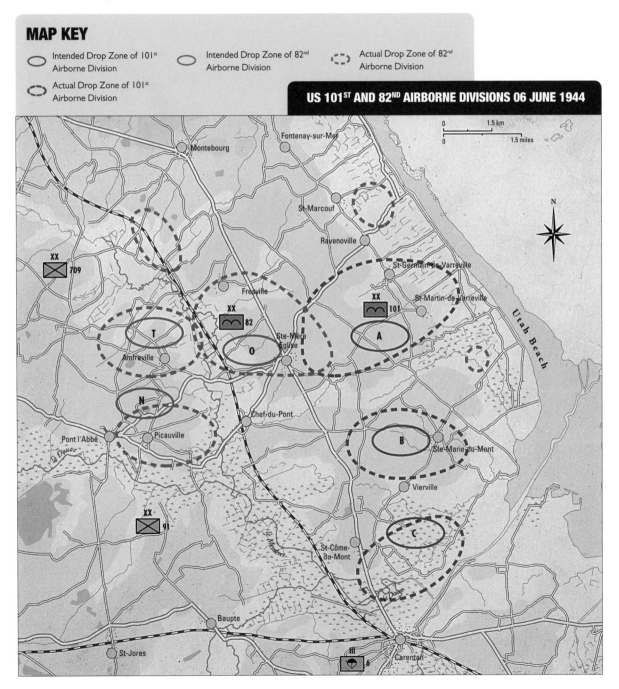

MAP KEY

Intended Drop Zone of 101st Airborne Division

Intended Drop Zone of 82nd Airborne Division

Actual Drop Zone of 82nd Airborne Division

Actual Drop Zone of 101st Airborne Division

US 101ST AND 82ND AIRBORNE DIVISIONS 06 JUNE 1944

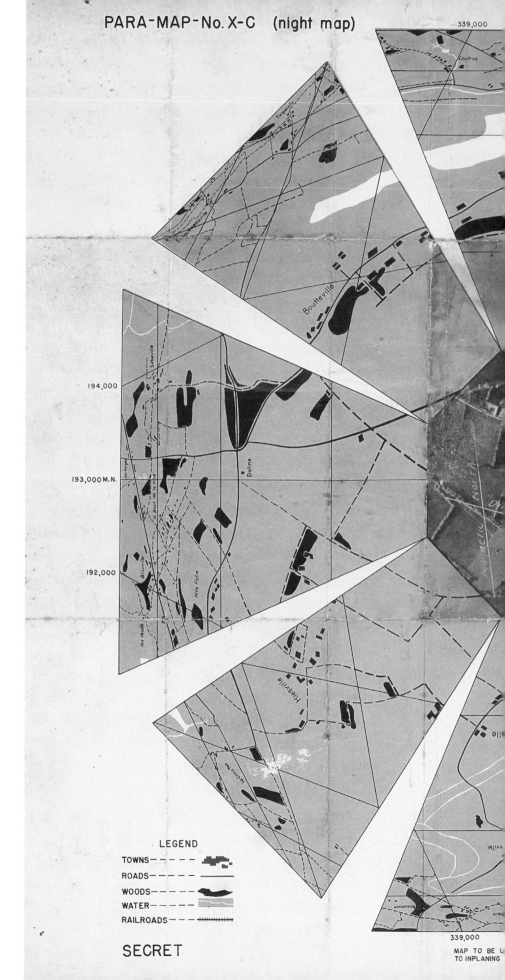

RIGHT: Paratroopers
eye-view jump map
of the drop zone at
Ste-Marie-du-Mont.
The town lay in
the planned drop
zone for the 101st
Airborne Division,
between Utah Beach
and Carentan to the
south. The map's
central octagonal
section is an aerial
reconnaissance
photograph.

46/47

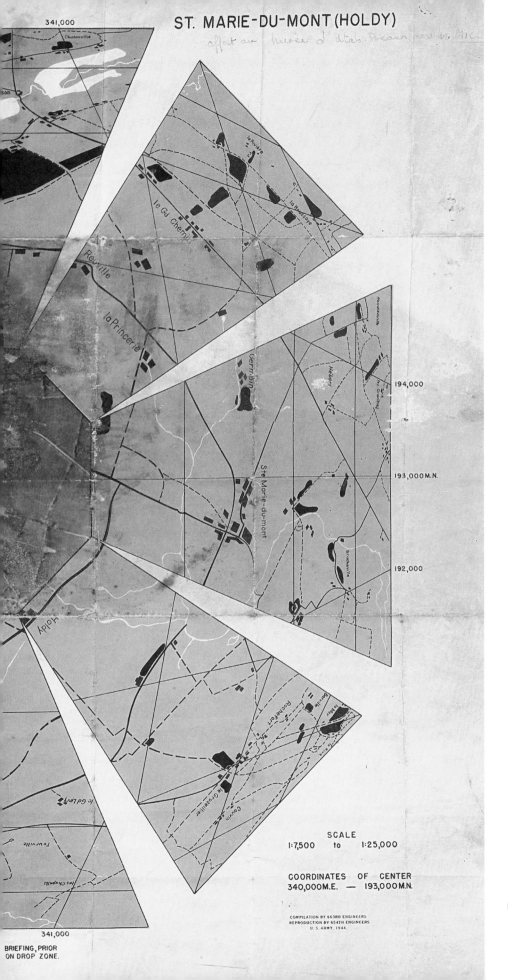

ST. MARIE-DU-MONT (HOLDY)

SCALE
1:7,500   to   1:25,000

COORDINATES OF CENTER
340,000 M.E. — 193,000 M.N.

COMPILATION BY 663RD ENGINEERS
REPRODUCTION BY 654TH ENGINEERS
U. S. ARMY, 1944.

BRIEFING, PRIOR
ON DROP ZONE.

TUESDAY 06 JUNE

UTAH BEACH

Bad weather had already caused the postponement of the invasion by one day, and D-Day itself was launched in what Eisenhower's chief meteorologist hoped would be a brief but usable window in the weather.

Conditions were very unpleasant in landing craft as they wallowed in the swell, and visibility was so poor that the bombers sent to provide last-minute softening-up of the defences at Utah and Omaha were largely ineffective. The landings were to take place after low water on a rising tide, and local conditions meant that they would begin at 6.30 am in the US sector and 7.30 am in the British. Fast German patrol boats alerted at about 3.30 am, attacked the invasion flotilla (the only serious casualty was the Norwegian destroyer *Svenner*) and at 5.35 am, only 15 minutes before Allied warships began their own bombardment, German coastal batteries began to open fire.

Although the overriding importance of the deep-water port of Cherbourg always made it desirable for a landing to take place at the base of the Cotentin, it was only when the original Cossac plan was modified early in 1944 to involve a five-division assault that planners were able to add Utah Beach to their schedule. Even then it was not ideal, for it was separated by rivers from the other beaches, and the low ground behind it had been flooded, restricting the routes inland. Major General Raymond Barton's 4th Division of VII Corps was to land there on a two-battalion front, with 36 Duplex Drive (DD) swimming tanks supporting the first wave.

PREVIOUS PAGE: American troops in foxholes on Utah while beach clearance goes on in the background.

RIGHT: A US soldier, carrying the light .30 M1 Carbine, moves along Utah Beach.

BELOW: American infantrymen crossing the sea wall and the dunes behind it: the gradient here is far gentler than at Omaha.

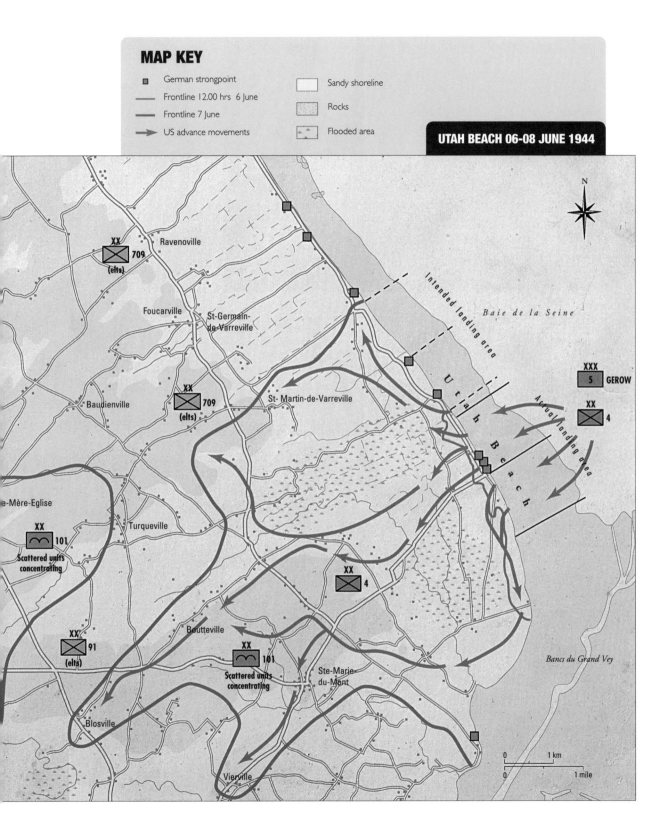

MAP KEY

- ■ German strongpoint
- —— Frontline 12.00 hrs 6 June
- —— Frontline 7 June
- ➤ US advance movements

- ☐ Sandy shoreline
- ▦ Rocks
- ▨ Flooded area

UTAH BEACH 06-08 JUNE 1944

N

Ravenoville

XX 709 (elts)

Foucarville

St-Germain-de-Varreville

Baie de la Seine

Intended landing area

XXX 5 GEROW

Baudienville

XX 709 (elts)

St-Martin-de-Varreville

U t a h   B e a c h

XX 4

Actual landing area

-Mère-Eglise

XX 101
Scattered units concentrating

Turqueville

XX 4

XX 91 (elts)

Boutteville

XX 101
Scattered units concentrating

Ste-Marie-du-Mont

Bancs du Grand Vey

Blosville

0   1 km

0   1 mile

Vierville

UTAH BEACH

THEODORE ROOSEVELT JR

Son of the president of the same name, and a brigadier general, he served in the First World War and helped create the American Legion after it. He distinguished himself as assistant division commander of 4th Infantry Division on D-Day, but died of a heart attack on 12 July, the day he was due to take command of his own division. Awarded the Congressional Medal of Honor, America's highest gallantry award, he lies buried at St-Laurent, beside his brother Quentin, killed in 1918.

ABOVE: The watch worn on D-Day by Staff Sergeant Glen E. Gibson of the 70th Tank Battalion. Gibson was the sole survivor from the crews of four amphibious tanks which were destroyed when their landing craft hit a mine off Utah Beach. His watch was stopped by the explosion at 5.46 am.

LEFT: US Army-issue Bible carried into battle on Utah Beach in the breast pocket of Staff Sergeant Louie Havard. During D-Day an enemy bullet struck Havard's rifle, ricocheted off it and struck the Bible, which saved his life. Louie Havard survived the Second World War.

RIGHT: US 4th Infantry Division.

There was good luck and bad. A mixture of a strong coastal current and the obscuration of navigation landmarks by the smoke of the naval bombardment meant that the whole invasion force landed about 2,000 yards further south than had been planned, and the tanks arrived late. But the area where the troops came ashore, around La Grande Dune, was actually much less heavily defended than the planned attack sector, and casualties on the run-in and the landing itself were mercifully light. There might have been confusion as junior commanders realized that they were in the wrong place, but the assistant division commander, the arthritic but dogged Brigadier General Theodore Roosevelt (son of the president of the same name), had pressed to be allowed to go ashore with the first wave. Under fire most of the day, he repeatedly led groups over the sea wall and pointed them inland. His bravery earned him the Congressional Medal of Honor, and helped ensure that within three hours of the first landing the beach was secure and cleared, with engineers and naval demolition parties dealing with beach obstacles, making gaps in the sea wall and clearing minefields. By nightfall infantry had pushed as far inland as the main Cherbourg–Bayeux road at Les Forges.

PLANNED H-HOUR: 06.30

ALLIES

Assaulting Division: US 4th Infantry
Division Commander:
Major General Raymond O. Barton
Infantry Assault Units: 1st and 2nd
Battalions of the 8th Infantry Regiment
Men Landed: 23,250
Casualties (dead, wounded & missing): c.200

AXIS

Defending Divisions: Elements of 709th
Infantry and 352nd Infantry
709TH Infantry Division Commander:
Lieutenant General Karl-Wilhelm von Schlieben
352ND Infantry Division Commander:
Lieutenant General Dietrich Kraiss

Many thanks — from the 323rd Bomb Group, which flew over Utah Beach on D-Day, see the Bud Hutton article.

THE STARS AND STRIPES

1D **1D**

Daily Newspaper of U.S. Armed Forces — in the European Theater of Operations

Vol. 4 No. 185 — New York, N.Y.—London, England — Wednesday, June 7, 1944

Allies Driving Into France

Opposition Less Than Expected; Troops 10 Mi. In

Allied armies, supported by more than 4,000 ships and 11,000 warplanes, stormed the northern coast of France in the dark hours of yesterday morning to open the decisive battle for the liberation of Europe, and by nightfall had smashed their way ten miles inland to Caen, between the French ports of Cherbourg and Le Havre. Enemy radio stations said heavy street fighting was in progress.

By reaching Caen, the invasion forces may have cut the railway running from Paris to Cherbourg, main route for the supply of Hitler's troops on the peninsula.

German opposition in all quarters—sea, air and land—was less than expected, according to information reaching supreme headquarters and losses appeared to be astonishingly light.

American naval losses were only two destroyers and one LST (landing ship, tank) craft, while American air losses were kept to one per cent, President Roosevelt revealed in Washington on the basis of a noon dispatch from General Eisenhower. The President said operations were "up to schedule."

Losses of troop-carrying aircraft were extremely small, although more than 1,000 of such planes were used, headquarters disclosed. The airborne troops themselves were "well established," Prime Minister Churchill had announced earlier.

And as for the forces which landed on the beaches, Adm. Sir Bertram Ramsay, Allied naval commander-in-chief, reported that "naval ships landed all their cargoes 100 per cent." He added that there was "slight loss in ships, but so slight that it did not affect putting armies ashore. We have got all the first wave of men through the defended beach zone and set for the land battle."

Along a front described by the Germans as 80 miles long—from the mouth of the Seine River at Le Havre to the tip of the Cherbourg peninsula—American, British and Canadian troops landed on French soil from the choppy waters of the English Channel and from the storm-studded skies.

From 600 naval guns, ranging from four to 16 inches, and from massive fleets of supporting planes, ton upon ton of high explosives thundered into the concrete and steel of the West Wall which Hitler erected to guard his conquered countries.

The actual landings took place in daylight after an aerial assault on the coastal defenses which lasted from before midnight to dawn, a communique disclosed late last night. The airborne troops, however, had landed behind enemy positions during darkness.

Between 6.30 and 7.30 two naval task forces—one commanded by Rear Adm. Sir Philip Vian, aboard HMS Scylla, and the other by Rear Adm. Alan Goodrich Kirk, aboard the U.S.S. Augusta—launched their assault forces at enemy beaches.

It was on the cruiser Augusta that President Roosevelt and Prime Minister Churchill signed the Atlantic Charter in August, 1941.

The mightiest air and sea armadas ever assembled paved the way for the successful landings. American warships participating included battleships, cruisers and destroyers, as well as hundreds of smaller craft and troopships.

Thirty-one thousand Allied airmen, not counting airborne troops, made a continuous road through the night in the skies over France. Between midnight and 8 AM more than 10,000 tons of high explosives were hurled upon the Normandy invasion area by Allied aircraft, which flew 7,500 sorties.

Against this aerial might the Luftwaffe was able to mount only 50 sorties, despite an order of the day from Goering that "invasion must be beaten off even if the Luftwaffe perishes." Allied fighters swept 75 miles inland without opposition.

After an initial communique made the momentous announcement of the landings, Prime Minister Churchill gave the first word that the assault had been successful. To a cheering House of Commons he announced shortly after noon that landings were proceeding according to plan, that sea obstacles planted by the Nazis had been largely quelled, and that airborne landings had been effected successfully behind the enemy lines.

Later, after visiting Gen. Eisenhower's headquarters with King George VI, Churchill said that "many dangers and difficulties which appeared at this time last night to be extremely formidable are behind us. The passage of the sea has been made with far less loss than we apprehended."

A spokesman at Supreme Headquarters Allied Expeditionary Forces (SHAEF) declared last night that the "first four or five hurdles" in establishing Allied forces on the Continent had been overcome, and that the positions of the Allied troops definitely gave "no cause for pessimism." No specific information was given on the landing points or the progress made.

It was left to the Germans to give most of the details, and all day long came a steady stream of reports from German agencies of new airborne and sea landings, most of them between Le Havre and

Cherbourg and some airborne landings southwest of Boulogne.

Enemy radio stations late last night painted a picture of growing Allied successes, with new beachheads established and a general spreading-out from positions on coastal stretches already occupied.

German Overseas News Agency said tierce fighting was in progress along the whole 19-mile stretch of road between Carentan and Valognes on the Cherbourg peninsula. Paratroops established themselves on both sides of the road and later were reinforced by glider troops, the agency added.

Vichy radio said Allied reinforcements were pouring into the beachheads and "it must be admitted the Allied landing area has been considerably extended."

The French radio station at Brazza-

(Continued on page 4)

Late Bulletins

FIRST U.S. RAID FROM USSR BASES

U.S. BOMBER BASE, Soviet Union, June 6 (Reuter)—In the first American raid of the war from new shuttle bases on Soviet soil, scores of U.S. heavy bombers showered tons of high explosives and incendiaries on airdrome installations at Galatz, Rumania, today and then returned here.

STALIN LAUDS ALLIES ON ROME

A congratulatory message from Marshal Stalin on "the great victory of the Allied Anglo-American forces" at Rome was made public last night by Prime Minister Churchill. Stalin wrote that the news of Rome capture was "greeted in the Soviet Union with great satisfaction."

INVASION JAMS U.S. PAPERS

WASHINGTON, June 6 (Reuter)—Many newspapers announced tomorrow's editions would not contain advertising because of pressure of space,

Greatest Umbrella for Landing

Armadas of Allied Planes Hammer Nazi Targets

Unleashing the full fury of Anglo-American air power, Allied aircraft yesterday bombed and strafed mile after mile of French beaches, seizing undisputed mastery of the air and heaping record-breaking tons of explosives on Nazi coastal installations in providing the greatest umbrella in history for the invasion forces.

Between midnight and 8 AM yesterday alone, 10,000 tons of steel went cascading down on German targets on the coast of Normandy. In the same period more than 31,000 Allied airmen, not including airborne troops, dominated the sky over France.

It was estimated that in a final capitulation the number of sorties flown yesterday would soar to more than 20,000.

In spite of the staggering number of sorties flown by the Americans only 1 per cent of the aircraft operating were lost, President Roosevelt announced in Washington at noon.

Luftwaffe Stays Down

So sparse was Luftwaffe opposition that most airmen did not encounter a single German fighter. Few of the 1,750 fighter planes which it is estimated the Nazis can muster to oppose the invasion put in an appearance.

High-ranking officers of Supreme Headquarters emphasized, however, that there was no reason to believe the Luftwaffe had been defeated.

"Fighting of the greatest severity is in store before the Luftwaffe is wiped out," according to one air officer.

American heavies, flying three missions for the second time in four days, roared out at 6 AM, at noon and again in the mid-afternoon at a cost of only four bombers.

In the first assault a record force of more than 1,300 Fortresses and Liberators struck more than 100 German targets on the French coast. Later in the day a medium force of B24s and B17s flew behind the West Wall to pound a defended German position. Most of the bombers in the second raid returned with their loads because the presence of Allied troops made it inadvisable to bomb through overcast. Another Nazi strongpoint was battered on the third mission.

Not one enemy fighter was encountered.

Bombing, strafing and patrolling fighter aircraft of the Ninth Air Force were in the air continuously yesterday from 4.30 AM, covering the movement of the Allied Expeditionary Force over sea and on to the beaches, and probing ahead of the landing parties for tactical objectives beyond the operations zone.

Starting yesterday morning with air-

(Continued on page 3)

'This Was the Invasion'

Flying S & S Writer Files First Eyewitness Story

By Bud Hutton
Stars and Stripes Staff Writer

Six thousand feet below, troops surged over the beaches of France and against Hitler's Atlantic Wall, and as the first black dots moved over the white sand a gunner said over the interphone: "Jesus Christ! At last."

On the dirty dark green of the Channel waters, battleships, cruisers, destroyers and more man-carrying craft than you could count rolled steadily toward the green fields and the white towns the Nazis had taken from France. Through a smoke screen the wraith-like shapes of warships loomed a moment, chameleoned into blobs of flame as another broadside roared off to find some Wehrmacht strongpoint beyond the coast.

This was the invasion.

North and south, all across the Channel and deep into the reaches beyond the concrete-bound coasts of the Continent, some 7,000 American and Allied warplanes flew in the greatest aerial armada in history. They dived the Luftwaffe from the skies with guns, and with bombs the German gunners and infantry from their camouflaged strongpoints beneath.

It was the Marauders and Havocs, Fortresses and Liberators, Mustangs, Thunderbolts, Lightnings and all the myriad craft of the RAF filled the sky until there was no room for more.

From a Marauder medium bomber of

(Continued on page 4)

Teheran Set Landing Time With Stalin's OK, Says FDR

WASHINGTON, June 6—President Roosevelt disclosed today that the approximate invasion time was set at the Teheran conference last December and that Marshal Stalin was completely satisfied with it. The precise date, however, was determined only within the last few days.

Citing losses far fewer than expected, Mr. Roosevelt told his press conference that politicians who had been demanding a second front for months would see now why the Allies had waited—the extra time had enabled Gen. Eisenhower to have many more divisions and landing craft.

Eisenhower's Order of Day

The following order of the day was issued yesterday by Gen. Eisenhower to each individual of the Allied Expeditionary Force:

"Soldiers, sailors and airmen of the Allied Expeditionary Force!

"You are about to embark upon the great crusade, toward which we have striven these many months. The eyes of the world are upon you. The hopes and prayers of liberty-loving people everywhere march with you.

"In company with our brave allies and brothers in arms on other fronts, you will bring about the destruction of the German war machine, the elimination of Nazi tyranny over the oppressed peoples of Europe, and security for ourselves in a free world.

"Your task will not be an easy one. Your enemy is well trained, well equipped and battle hardened. He will fight savagely.

"But this is the year 1944! Much has happened since the Nazi triumphs of 1940-41. The United Nations have inflicted upon the Germans great defeats in open battle, man to man. Our air offensive has seriously reduced their strength in the air and their capacity to wage war on the ground.

"Our home fronts have given us an overwhelming superiority in weapons and munitions of war, and placed at our disposal great reserves of trained fighting men. The tide has turned! The free men of the world are marching together to victory!

"I have full confidence in your courage, devotion to duty and skill in battle. We will accept nothing less than full victory!

"Good luck! And let us beseech the blessing of Almighty God upon this great and noble undertaking."

The order was distributed to assault elements after their embarkation. It was read by commanders to all other troops in the Allied Expeditionary Force.

POINTE DU HOC

The Pointe du Hoc (Hoe in the US Official History – the word stems from old French for a vessel's jib) was as important to the Americans as Pegasus Bridge and Merville were to the British.

The clifftop site, rising 177 feet from the shore, was believed to house six 155mm guns in concrete emplacements: they could either fire onto Utah Beach or at the force assaulting Omaha. These defences had been damaged by bombing, but aerial and naval bombardment could not guarantee to destroy them. Their location meant that neither parachutists nor glider troops could be used, and the mission was given to Lieutenant Colonel James E. Rudder's 2nd Ranger Battalion, which would storm from the sea.

Colonel Rudder's first wave of three companies would land at the foot of the cliffs, scale them, and then be reinforced by another two companies, while his 6th company continued to Omaha, whence it would join the rest of the battalion by land. Most of the Rangers would be in landing craft, but four amphibious DUKWs, fitted with turntable ladders supplied by the London Fire Brigade, mounted twin Lewis machine guns. To climb the cliffs, ropes attached to grapnels were to be fired by special projectors.

ABOVE: A-20s of the US Ninth Air Force attacking the Pointe du Hoc (bottom right) on D-Day.

BELOW: The battleship USS *Texas* pounding the Pointe du Hoc with her 14-inch guns on D-Day. She formed part of the Western Task Force under Rear Admiral D. P. Kirk, USN.

JAMES EARL RUDDER

A college teacher and football coach with a reserve commission, Rudder was called to active duty in 1941. He took command of 2nd Ranger Battalion in 1942, leading it in its assault on the Pointe du Hoc. Rudder was a full colonel in 1945, and subsequently combined careers as university president, civic leader and reserve officer, rising to major general. President Johnson awarded him the Distinguished Service Medal, the highest peacetime service award, in 1967.

BELOW: 2nd Ranger Batalion

Rudder's men transferred to their landing craft and DUKWs 12 miles out, lost two craft in heavy seas, and lost two more when they ran in parallel to the coast after making the wrong landfall. Although the garrison was ready for them, the Rangers began their ascent at once, undaunted by the fact that waterlogged ropes prevented the grapnels from rising far enough. A last-minute attack by B-26 bombers rattled the defenders, and the destroyers USS Satterlee and HMS Talybont fired as the Rangers climbed. There were no guns in the casemates – they had been moved inland to escape the bombing, but Rudder's men found and destroyed them. The Rangers were then counter-attacked and forced back into the original German defences, but they held until relieved on 8 June. They lost 135 of the 225 men landed: the follow-up companies did not receive the success signal and went on to Omaha.

LEFT: Allied bombing and naval gunfire had done terrible damage to German defences before the Rangers landed.

PLANNED H-HOUR: 06.30

ALLIES

Assaulting Units: D, E and F Companies of 2nd Ranger Battalion
Commander: Lieutenant Colonel James E. Rudder
Men Landed: 225
Casualties: 135 (by 8 June 1944)

AXIS

Defending Unit: Elements of 716TH Coastal Defence Division
Number: 200
716TH Coastal Defence Division Commander: Lieutenant General Wilhelm Richter

LEFT: An Allied secret briefing map showing the German defensive positions on the Pointe du Hoc in April 1944.

RIGHT: This aerial reconnaissance photograph of Pointe du Hoc (the point itself is at the top of the photograph) gives a good view of the damage done by bombing before D-Day. The map overlay is a detail from the map on the left.

585

587

O.R., SEE
SKETCH

TRENCHES

GUN POSITIONS
DISMANTLED →

COVERED
TRENCH

4.

3.

2.

6.

5864 9381
ELEV. ABOVE
M.S.L. 115'

BLDG. REMOVED

WIRE

OMAHA BEACH

Omaha was the responsibility of the US V Corps. Major General Clarence R. Huebner's 1st Division would land with two regiments abreast, the 116th Infantry (from the 29th Division) on the right and the 16th Infantry on the left. Once the beach was secured, these regiments would be supported by two other regiments, and the attackers would then seize the Bayeux road to the south and perhaps reach Isigny to the west.

The beach's gentle-sloping sand led to coarse shingle, and immediately behind rose high sandy bluffs. There were only five exits through them, and these valleys ("draws" to their attackers) were protected by concrete bunkers. Nowhere else were assaulting troops confronted with such serious obstacles. The area was defended by the over-extended 716th Division (responsible for the coastline from the Orne to the west of Omaha), but at Omaha it had been reinforced by the higher-quality 352nd Division, undetected by Allied intelligence. While the British had placed emphasis on getting specialist armoured vehicles ashore at the very beginning to deal with obstacles, the American approach was less technological, and beach-clearing was to be done by unarmoured engineer teams. Lastly, the long run-in through heavy seas caused losses before the attackers reached the shore, and the coastal current meant that most landing craft beached eastwards of their intended landfall.

At 5.40 am the first DD tanks were launched 6,000 yards out, but most foundered at once, and of the 32 only five reached the

shore, doing so after the assaulting infantry. The artillery expected to fire on the way in did little better: all but one of the 105mm guns of 11th Field Artillery Battalion were lost, as were six of 7th Field Artillery Battalion's pieces. Although naval bombardment had temporarily neutralized the defences, they came to life as the landing-craft neared the shoreline, and the nine companies of the first assaulting wave were disgorged – overloaded, soaking and often sea-sick – onto the surf of a bullet-swept beach. Undamaged obstacles gave them a degree of cover but posed a terrible risk to incoming DUKWs and landing craft.

The failure of the first wave meant that the specialist engineer teams were unable to work as planned, despite suffering 40 per cent casualties that day. After the first dreadful hour the

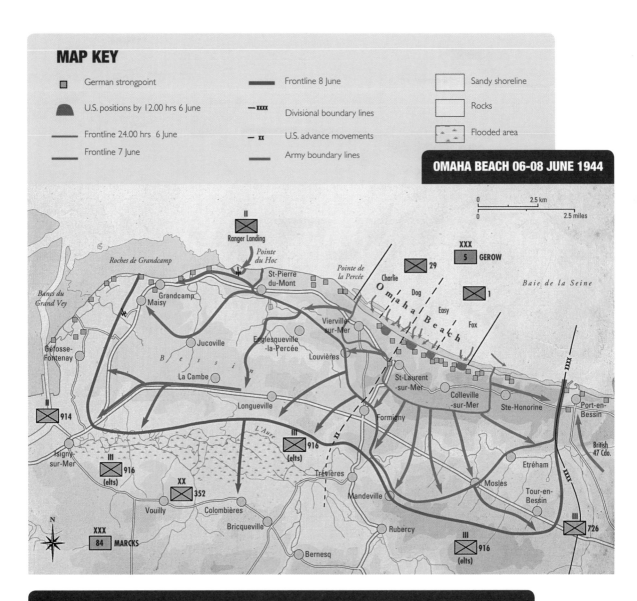

MAP KEY

- □ German strongpoint
- ◗ U.S. positions by 12.00 hrs 6 June
- ▬ Frontline 24.00 hrs 6 June
- ▬ Frontline 7 June
- ▬ Frontline 8 June
- – xxxx Divisional boundary lines
- – xx U.S. advance movements
- ▬ Army boundary lines
- ▢ Sandy shoreline
- ▢ Rocks
- ▨ Flooded area

OMAHA BEACH 06-08 JUNE 1944

0   2.5 km
0   2.5 miles

II Ranger Landing

Pointe du Hoc

Roches de Grandcamp

Banes du Grand Vey

St-Pierre du-Mont

Pointe de la Percée

Charlie Dog Easy Fox

XXX 5 GEROW

XX 29

XX 1

Baie de la Seine

Grandcamp Maisy

Géfosse-Fontenay

Jucoville

Englesqueville-la-Percée

Louvières

Vierville-sur-Mer

O m a h a   B e a c h

B e s s i n

La Cambe

St-Laurent-sur-Mer

Colleville-sur-Mer

Ste-Honorine

Port-en-Bessin

II 914

Longueville

L'Aure

III 916 (elts)

XX

Formigny

Moslés

Etréham

Tour-en-Bessin

British 47 Cdo.

Isigny-sur-Mer

III 916 (elts)

XX 352

Trévières

Mandeville

Rubercy

III 726

Vouilly

Colombières

Bricqueville

Bernesq

III 916 (elts)

XXX 84 MARCKS

N

PLANNED H-HOUR: 06.30

ALLIES

Assaulting Division: US 1st Infantry
US 1ST Division Commander:
  Major General Clarence R. Huebner
Infantry Assault Units:
  2nd and 3rd Battalions of the 16th Infantry Regiment,
  and 1st and 2nd Battalions of the 116th Infantry
  Regiment attached from US 29th Infantry Division
Men Landed: 34,250
Casualties (dead, wounded & missing): c.3,000

AXIS

Defending Divisions:
  Elements of 352nd Infantry and 716th
Coastal
  Defence
352ND Infantry Division Commander:
  Lieutenant General Dietrich Kraiss
716TH Coastal Defence Division Commander:
  Lieutenant General Wilhelm Richter

OPPOSITE RIGHT:
The Purple
Heart, for all
US personnel
wounded or
killed in combat.
Around 3,000
were awarded
to the D-Day
casualties on
Omaha.

116th Infantry had a toehold just west of Les Moulins, and, as much by luck as by judgement, it was there that the regimental command group under Colonel Charles D. W. Canham and the assistant division commander, Brigadier General Norman D. Cota, landed. The view from the sea was depressing: one officer reported that beach was clogged with infantry while landing craft milled about like "a stampeded herd of cattle". Lieutenant General Omar N. Bradley, the US First Army commander, aboard USS Augusta, even briefly considered redirecting the remaining units to Utah Beach.

By this time there was progress on the beach as destroyers came dangerously close inshore to engage defences at point-blank range, and determined groups of men fought their way off the beach. Sometimes they were formal leaders, and sometimes they were not: decorations honoured the achievements of Brigadier General Cota at one extreme and several gallant NCOs and private soldiers at the other. By the day's end the Americans held a narrow strip of land between St-Laurent and Colleville, but they lacked most of the resources needed for the planned advance inland. Omaha Beach had cost V Corps around 3,000 casualties, more than were suffered on the other beaches in total.

> "We hit the eye of the storm. The battalion was decimated. Hell, after that we didn't have enough to whip a cat with."
>
> SGT JOHN R. SLAUGHTER, D Co.,
> 116th Infantry Regiment, 29th Division

BELOW: The photographer Robert Capa landed at Omaha, but most of the film he shot was ruined by an over-enthusiastic developer. This photograph shows infantrymen moving through the surf and the beach defences.

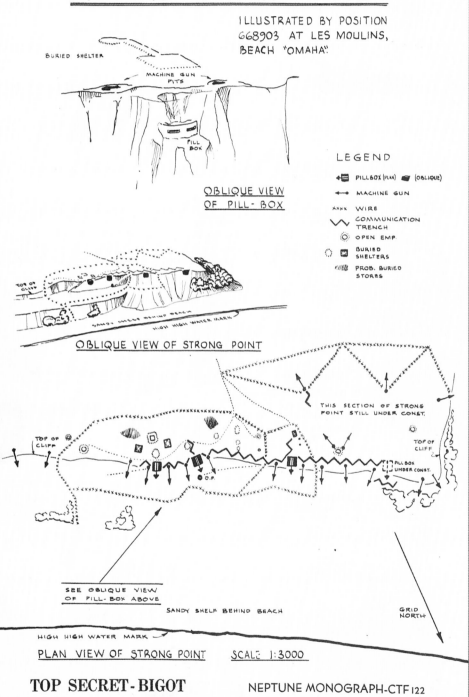

TYPICAL STRONG POINT

ILLUSTRATED BY POSITION 668903 AT LES MOULINS, BEACH "OMAHA".

BURIED SHELTER

MACHINE GUN PITS

PILL BOX

OBLIQUE VIEW OF PILL-BOX

LEGEND

PILLBOX (PLAN)   (OBLIQUE)

MACHINE GUN

XXXX   WIRE

COMMUNICATION TRENCH

OPEN EMP.

BURIED SHELTERS

PROB. BURIED STORES

TOP OF CLIFF

SANDY SHELF BEHIND BEACH

HIGH HIGH WATER MARK

OBLIQUE VIEW OF STRONG POINT

THIS SECTION OF STRONG POINT STILL UNDER CONST.

TOP OF CLIFF

TOP OF CLIFF

PILL BOX UNDER CONST.

O.P.

SEE OBLIQUE VIEW OF PILL-BOX ABOVE

SANDY SHELF BEHIND BEACH

GRID NORTH

HIGH HIGH WATER MARK

PLAN VIEW OF STRONG POINT   SCALE 1:3000

TOP SECRET - BIGOT   NEPTUNE MONOGRAPH - CTF 122

LEFT: US troops wade through thigh-high water, the pull of underwater current and ongoing German gunfire as they disembark from USS *Samuel Chase* onto the sector of Omaha Beach that they called Fox Green.

RIGHT: A page from top-secret Allied briefing documents, dated 21 April 1944, describing the key features of Omaha Beach, including type of sand, tides, landmarks, approaches, underwater obstacles, and natural and man-made defences.

Message Book M-105-A
Signal Corps, U. S. Army

16—20155

THESE SPACES FOR MESSAGE CENTER ONLY

TIME FILED | MSG CEN No. | HOW SENT

MESSAGE
(CLASSIFICATION) (SUBMIT TO MESSAGE CENTER IN DUPLICATE)

NO _____ 10 _____ DATE _____
To _____ LTG _____

From one thousand yds
off Red Beach I see
several companies one six
Inf on Easy Red and fox
red Beaches X enemy
artillery and Machine gun
fire still effective X Love
charlie Tares shifting from
Dog X about thirty
CT standing by to land

OFFICIAL DESIGNATION OF SENDER | TIME SIGNED

SIGNATURE AND GRADE OF WRITER

GPO 16—20155

THESE SPACES FOR MESSAGE CENTER ONLY

TIME FILED | MSG CEN No. | HOW SENT

MESSAGE
(CLASSIFICATION) (SUBMIT TO MESSAGE CENTER IN DUPLICATE)

NO _____ DATE _____
To 10 cont'd
Rifle and Obstacles
seem thicker than in
photos X Bty Able seven
FA in Dukws just arrived
X Love charlie item
eight five hit and
smoking after unloading
X have seen Two Love
charlie Tares Burn
Count Ten Tanks on
Fox X landing resuming
on Dog

OFFICIAL DESIGNATION OF SENDER | TIME SIGNED

SIGNATURE AND GRADE OF WRITER

GPO 16—20155

THESE SPACES FOR MESSAGE CENTER ONLY

TIME FILED | MSG CEN No. | HOW SENT

MESSAGE
(CLASSIFICATION) (SUBMIT TO MESSAGE CENTER IN DUPLICATE)

NO _____ 21 _____ DATE _____
To _____ LTG _____

Troops moving up slope
Fox Green and Fox Red X BBT X
I join you thanking God
for our Navy.

OFFICIAL DESIGNATION OF SENDER | TIME SIGNED

SIGNATURE AND GRADE OF WRITER

GPO 16—20155

THESE SPACES FOR MESSAGE CENTER ONLY

TIME FILED | MSG CEN No. | HOW SENT

MESSAGE
(CLASSIFICATION) (SUBMIT TO MESSAGE CENTER IN DUPLICATE)

NO _____ 23 _____ DATE _____
To _____ LTG _____

Enemy artillery registered
on beach easy Red and
fires when craft are
there X Believe craft can
be seen from church spire
at Vierville

OFFICIAL DESIGNATION OF SENDER | 1205 TIME SIGNED

SIGNATURE AND GRADE OF WRITER

GPO 16—20155

630

THESE SPACES FOR MESSAGE CENTER ONLY

TIME FILED Urgent | MSG CEN No. | HOW SENT

MESSAGE
(CLASSIFICATION) (SUBMIT TO MESSAGE CENTER IN DUPLICATE)

NO _____ DATE _____
To

Arrived on beach eight
zero X X Situation diff-
icult X Information limited
X progress slow X From Wyman
to Heubner X Liaison
with combat units only X
Radio out X Wire going
in at present. BBT sends

OFFICIAL DESIGNATION OF SENDER | 1347 TIME SIGNED

SIGNATURE AND GRADE OF WRITER

GPO 16—20155

NORMAN "DUTCH" COTA

was an ebullient New Englander. Assistant division commander of the 29th Division, he was the first general ashore on Omaha Beach. Showing characteristic vigour in getting men off the beach, he shouted to one group of soldiers that, as Rangers, they should be leading the way. Promoted to command the 28th Division, he led it through Paris in the liberation parade, and in heavy fighting in the Hürtgen Forest. His division was badly mauled in the German Ardennes offensive.

OPPOSITE: D-Day situation report messages sent by the US Information Team on Omaha Beach, led by Colonel B.B. Talley, to Major General Leonard T. Gerow ("LTG"), US V Corps Commander, who was watching developments from a ship offshore. All 21 officers and men of the Information Team were decorated for gallantry on D-Day, one of the largest single-unit awards in US Army history.

RIGHT: A medic tends a wounded man on Omaha. Note the drip held by his assistant: promptly administered, intravenous saline replacements were invaluable in reducing deaths from shock.

GOLD BEACH

Gold, the westernmost of the British/Canadian beaches, was to be assaulted by Major General D. A. H. Graham's 50th Division of XXX Corps, which was to advance to take Bayeux, and hook right to capture Arromanches (where the British Mulberry harbour was to be built) and then link up with the Americans.

50th Division had begun the war as a Territorial formation recruited from the north-east (its distinctive divisional flash bore TT, for Tyne-Tees), and it had fought in France in 1940 and subsequently in the Western Desert. Its regional composition had been much diluted and, sadly, dwindling numbers of British soldiers available for service in the infantry were eventually to result in its disbandment: but not before it added further lustre to its laurels on D-Day.

50th Division was to land with two brigades forward, 231st on the right and 69th on the left, with 56th Brigade following-up on the right and 151st on the left. The division had 8th Armoured Brigade under command, and this provided one regiment of DD tanks with each assaulting brigade, the Nottinghamshire Yeomanry on the right and the 4th/7th Dragoon Guards on the left. Once the beach was secure, 47th Royal Marine Commando would

> ## "It was a sobering sight as the Hampshires left their smaller infantry landing craft. ... men were dropping while still in shallow water, to be dragged forward by their mates and left on the sand, while their comrades ran on in a purposeful steady jog trot, which betrayed no sign of panic."
>
> Trooper Joe Minogue, The Westminster Dragoons

MAP KEY

▫	Area of strongest German resistance
●	German resistance points
♛	German battery
⚊	Mines
—	Front line at 12.00 hours

Abbreviations

Hants	Hampshire
Cdo	Commando
GH	Green Howards
EY	East Yorkshire

PREVIOUS PAGE: Infantry of a follow-up wave coming ashore from a landing craft near Ver-sur-Mer on Gold Beach.

RIGHT: Cromwell tanks of 4th County of London Yeomanry, then part of 7th Armoured Division, moving ashore from Gold Beach on 7 June.

GOLD BEACH 06 JUNE 1944 UP TO 12.00 HOURS

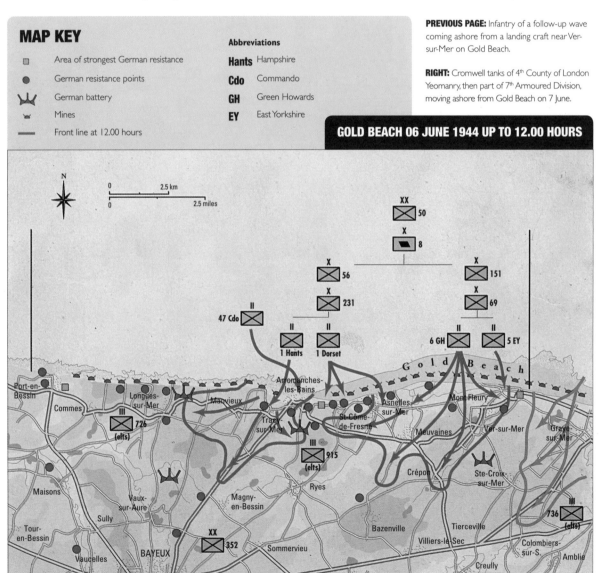

GOLD BEACH

land and make for Port-en-Bessin on the inter-Allied boundary. In contrast to American policy, specialist armoured vehicles, of the Westminster Dragoons and 6th Assault Regiment Royal Engineers, were to land just ahead of the infantry to deal with beach obstacles, mines and the sea wall. On Gold Beach alone there were almost 2,500 obstacles of one sort or another, embodying almost 900 tons of steel, concrete or wood.

Strong defences at Le Hamel briefly held up 231st Brigade – 1st Hampshire lost its commanding officer and second-in-command – but by 8.30 the whole brigade was ashore and making progress. On the left, 69th Brigade also ran into resistance just behind the beach, but the garrisons of a battery on Mont Fleury and the village of Ver-sur-Mer had been so cowed by naval and air

bombardment that they offered little opposition. With the assaulting brigades ashore, naval beachmasters began to organize the beaches so that follow-up units could land smoothly: 151st Brigade arrived at about 11.00, with 69th Brigade not far behind. By the day's end almost 25,000 men had gone ashore.

Progress inland was encouraging. The commandos dug in overlooking Port-en-Bessin, and Arromanches was cleared by nightfall. During the advance of 69th Brigade, Company Sergeant Major Stan Hollis of the Green Howards earned the Victoria Cross, the only one awarded as a result of D-Day, for valour that began on Mont Fleury and ended in the village of Crepon. By nightfall 151st Brigade had reached the Bayeux-Caen road. Bayeux itself was hopelessly exposed, and fell the following day.

PLANNED H-HOUR: 07.25

ALLIES

Assaulting Division: British 50th Division
Division Commander: Major General D.A.H. Graham
Infantry Assault Units:
1st Battalion Hampshire Regiment, 1st Battalion Dorset
    Regiment, 5th Battalion East Yorkshire
Regiment, 6th Battalion The Green Howards
First-Wave DD Tanks: Nottinghamshire Yeomanry, 4th/7th
Royal Dragoon Guards
Men Landed: 24,970
Casualties (dead, wounded & missing): c.400

AXIS

Defending Divisions:
Elements of 716th Coastal Defence and 352nd Infantry
716TH Coastal Defence Division Commander:
Lieutenant General Wilhelm Richter
352ND Infantry Division Commander:
Lieutenant General Dietrich Kraiss

ABOVE: British 50th Infantry Division

ABOVE: British 8th Armoured Brigade

ABOVE: British 231st Infantry Brigade.

OPPOSITE: British Sherman tanks move through the town of Bayeux, captured on 7 June. The first major French town to be liberated, Bayeux fell without much resistance. It was spared the terrible damage visited on Caen and St-Lô.

STAN HOLLIS

Hollis was a company sergeant major in 6th Green Howards, a Yorkshire Territorial battalion, on D-Day. He personally cleared German bunkers on Mont Fleury, and later attacked a field gun in the village of Crepon. Hollis was awarded the Victoria Cross, Britain's highest award for military bravery: it was the only one given for D-Day. The citation referred to his "utmost gallantry". After the war Hollis ran a pub, and told his wife to sell his VC when he died because it was, in effect, his pension.

GOLD BEACH

JUNO BEACH

Canada made a distinctive contribution to the Allied effort in both world wars, and it was fitting that Major General R. F. L. Keller's 3rd Canadian Division, part of I Corps, should land on Juno Beach.

The Canadian armed forces reflected, not without tensions, Canada's cultural divide: though most units serving overseas bore English titles and contained a majority of English-speaking men, Le Régiment de Maisonneuve and Les Fusiliers Mont-Royal, for example, were to play their part alongside the Black Watch of Canada and the South Saskatchewan Regiment in Normandy. Two Canadian destroyers, HMCS *Sioux* and *Algonquin*, were among the warships bombarding Juno, and they reflected the Canadian navy's costly service escorting Atlantic convoys.

ABOVE: Canadian infantrymen of Le Régiment de la Chaudière, the follow-up battalion of 8th Canadian Brigade, landing near Bernières on the morning of D-Day.

RIGHT: Canadian 3rd Infantry Division

The attack was complicated by the fact that the coast was protected by offshore rocks, exposed at low tide, except at the mouth of the River Seulles and the small port of Courseulles, where the Germans had thickened their defences. The town was the objective of 7th Canadian Brigade, the division's right assault brigade, while 8th Canadian Brigade was to land further east, at Bernières and St-Aubin-sur-Mer. Each assaulting brigade comprised three infantry battalions and an armoured regiment. As on British beaches, specialist armour, in this case from the 22nd Dragoons and 5th and 6th Assault Regiments Royal Engineers, was to deal with the beach defences. 9th Canadian Brigade would follow 8th onto the beaches. The defenders of Juno came from thinly spread 716th Division, which had about three companies – no more than 400

ABOVE: Men of 48 (Royal Marine) Commando going ashore on Nan, the easternmost sector of Juno Beach.

OPPOSITE: Letter from Canadian Lance Sergeant Edwin Owen Worden to his wife, written on the boat while waiting to cross the Channel on 5 June. Worden served with the 1st Battalion, Regina Rifle Regiment. He survived D-Day but died in Holland during the Allied Advance in April 1945.

BELOW: A standard M4 Sherman tank with a revolving drum fitted to a frontally extended frame, known as a "flail tank" or "crab". The chains attached to the drum exploded mines and cleared belts of barbed wire, leaving a safe path for following troops.

BOTTOM: A Duplex Drive (DD) Sherman tank with a collapsible canvas screen, which, when raised, gave it sufficient buoyancy to float. It had two propellers and a top speed in the water of over 4 knots. Amphibious armour was used for the first time on D-Day and gave the first-wave infantry invaluable fire support, which came as a complete surprise to the German defenders.

HOBART'S "FUNNIES"

Major General Sir Percy Hobart, brother-in-law of General Montgomery, was recalled from retirement in 1941, at the instigation of Winston Churchill, to take command of the 79th Armoured Division and mastermind the development of specially adapted armour to support a seaborne invasion. The "funnies", as they were known, were invaluable on Sword, Gold and Juno for facilitating rapid exit of the first waves of infantry and support vehicles off the beaches.

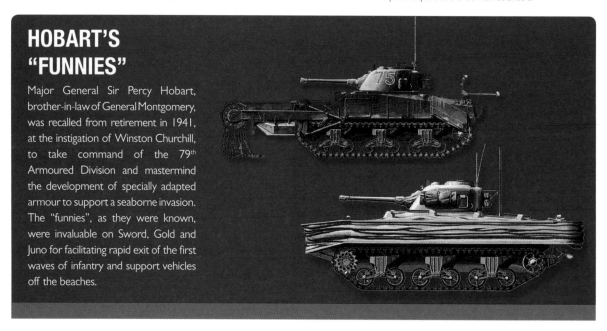

CANADIAN LEGION
WAR SERVICES Inc.

CANADIAN Y.M.C.A.
OVERSEAS

ON ACTIVE SERVICE

CANADIAN
KNIGHTS OF COLUMBUS
WAR SERVICES

THE SALVATION ARMY
CANADIAN
WAR SERVICES

L27027
Rfn E.O. Worden.
1st Bttn Regina Rifles
Can army England. Mon 5. 44

To my darling wife.
How are you to-night? fine
I hope. gee darling I find
it very hard to write
this to you. I only wish
I could have seen you. but
I can say this. I am fine.
and feel a 100 per cent. for
I know I have someone
waiting for me. who is
very brave and knows how
to smile.
We are going in to-
morrow morning. as I write
this we are out on the

CFA 170(4213)   PLEASE WRITE ON BOTH SIDES

CANADIAN LEGION
WAR SERVICES Inc.

CANADIAN Y.M.C.A.
OVERSEAS

ON ACTIVE SERVICE

CANADIAN
KNIGHTS OF COLUMBUS
WAR SERVICES

THE SALVATION ARMY
CANADIAN
WAR SERVICES

2

water. so the big day has
come. I often had wondered
how I would feel. but
I don't feel any
difference, as I ever did
befor. thanks to you. I
know I can
truthful say if it was
not for you I would
feel different. but it is
the love and trust I have
for you. and that will
help me over many a
rough spot.
I am glad in a way
that it has come. for it

CFA 170(4213)   PLEASE WRITE ON BOTH SIDES

CANADIAN LEGION
WAR SERVICES Inc.

CANADIAN Y.M.C.A.
OVERSEAS

ON ACTIVE SERVICE

CANADIAN
KNIGHTS OF COLUMBUS
WAR SERVICES

THE SALVATION ARMY
CANADIAN
WAR SERVICES

3

means you and I can be
togeather sooner. something
I have allways prayed
for. and I know you have
to. so promise darling
you will not worry. for
I'll be allright. and home
befor you know it.
Just you and mum look
after each other. and time
will pass swiftly.
Now befor I close I want
to say again. that I love
you very much and mean
the world to me.

CFA 170(4213)   PLEASE WRITE ON BOTH SIDES

So now darling I'll say
good-night and God bless
you till we meet again
soon
        yours forever.
            Love.
            Ted.
P.S. Tell mum that I am
thinking of her too. and
not to worry but look
after you.
I am encloseing a messag
they gave us. good-night
I'll write as soon as I
get a chance.

ABOVE: Sherman tanks of 3rd Canadian Armoured Brigade using an artificial trackway built by engineers to move up the beach: a sharp contrast to Dieppe.

BELOW: Anti-tank obstacles in the streets of St-Aubin-sur-Mer. The soldier taking cover from snipers is probably a member of the North Shore (New Brunswick) Regiment.

PLANNED H-HOUR: 07.45

ALLIES

Assaulting Division: Canadian 3rd Division
Division Commander: Major General R.F.L. Keller
Infantry Assault Units:
    The Royal Winnipeg Rifles, the Regina Rifle Regiment,
    the Queen's Own Rifles of Canada, the North Shore
    (New Brunswick) Regiment
First-Wave DD Tanks:
    6th Canadian Armoured Regiment, 10th Canadian
    Armoured Regiment
Men Landed: 21,500
Casualties (dead, wounded & missing): c.1,000

AXIS

Defending Division:
    Elements of 716th Coastal Defence Division
Division Commander:
    Lieutenant General Wilhelm Richter

men – in the path of an attack which would put 2,400 men and 76 tanks ashore in its first wave.

The Canadians landed slightly later than planned, which helped them get over the offshore rocks but meant that they arrived among beach defences. The landing craft had to jockey their way in and out among obstacles and 70 out of 306 were lost or damaged. Courseulles was stubbornly defended, and did not fall until well on in the afternoon, after Royal Marine Centaur tanks and Royal Engineer assault tanks supported the Royal Winnipeg Rifles and the Regina Rifles. Further east, the Queens Own Rifles suffered severely crossing the beach at Bernières, but soon stormed the village, and the New Brunswickers of the North Shore Regiment had a similar experience in St-Aubin. On the Canadian left, 48 (Royal Marine) Commando landing at about 9.00 am, lost landing craft to the now-submerged beach obstacles, and was galled by machine gun fire from St-Aubin, but swung left to capture Lagrune-sur-Mer, on the boundary with the British 3rd Division. Although the Canadians ended the day in contact with 50th Division on their right, and just short of the Bayeux-Caen road to their front, there remained a gap between them and Sword Beach on their left.

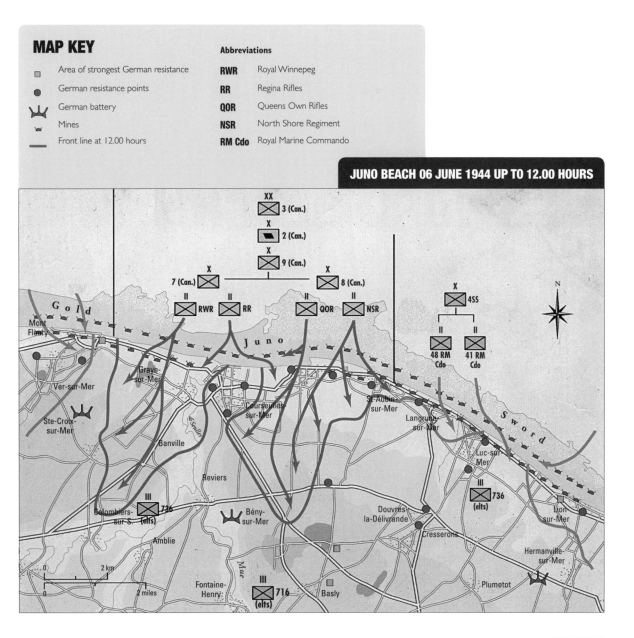

MAP KEY

- Area of strongest German resistance
- German resistance points
- German battery
- Mines
- Front line at 12.00 hours

Abbreviations

RWR	Royal Winnepeg
RR	Regina Rifles
QOR	Queens Own Rifles
NSR	North Shore Regiment
RM Cdo	Royal Marine Commando

JUNO BEACH 06 JUNE 1944 UP TO 12.00 HOURS

TUESDAY 06 JUNE

SWORD BEACH

Sword, the easternmost invasion beach, was the objective of Major General T. G. Rennie's 3rd Division. This division had fought (under Montgomery's command) in 1940, but had not been engaged since.

Its task was important and complex. Inland was the city of Caen, capital of Normandy and an important communication hub. Montgomery believed that its early capture was crucial because it would give him room for manoeuvre on the British flank. 3rd Division's orders specified that by nightfall it was to have "captured or effectively masked" the city. Next, the division had to facilitate a link with 6th Airborne Division via Pegasus Bridge, though the commandos of 1st Special Service Brigade, landing on the eastern edge of Sword Beach and taking Ouistreham, were going to make the junction. Finally, it was known that the only German armour close enough to launch a counter-attack, 21st Panzer Division, was in the area, so it was likely that 3rd Division would encounter German armour.

The presence of offshore rocks and the proximity of the mouth of the Orne and the town of Ouistreham meant that 3rd Division landed on the front of a single brigade, which made its deployment sequential rather than simultaneous. The leading brigade, 8th, used two of its battalions, 1st South Lancashire and 2nd East Yorkshire, to secure the coastal strip, and then pushed its third battalion, 1st Suffolk, assisted by tanks of the 13th/18th Hussars, inland to attack a German battery near Colleville and a strongpoint codenamed Hillman just

ABOVE: Commandos of Brigadier Lord Lovat's 1st Special Service Brigade, destined to relieve the paratroops at Pegasus Bridge, landing at La Brèche in the Queen Red sector.

PLANNED H-HOUR: 07.25

ALLIES

Assaulting Division: British 3rd Division
Division Commander: Major General T. G. Rennie
Infantry Assault Units: 1st South Lancashire Regiment,
    2nd East Yorkshire Regiment
First-Wave DD Tanks: 13th/18th Hussars
Men Landed: 28,845
Casualties (dead, wounded & missing): c.630

AXIS

Defending Division:
    Elements of 716th Coastal Defence Division
Division Commander:
    Lieutenant General Wilhelm Richter

> "I started the pipes up and marched up and down. This sergeant came running over, 'Get down you mad bastard. You're attracting attention on us.' Anyway I continued marching up and down until we moved off the beach."

Piper Bill Millin, 1st Special Service Brigade

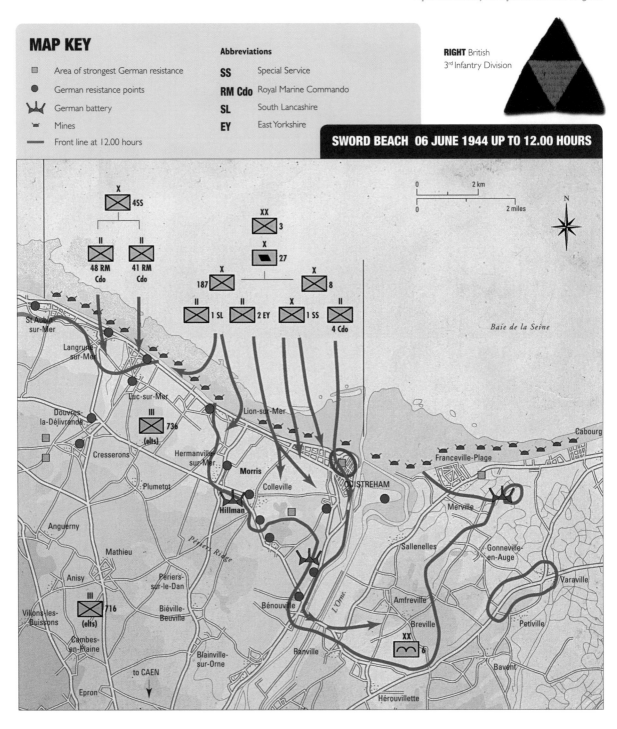

MAP KEY

- Area of strongest German resistance
- German resistance points
- German battery
- Mines
- Front line at 12.00 hours

Abbreviations

SS	Special Service
RM Cdo	Royal Marine Commando
SL	South Lancashire
EY	East Yorkshire

RIGHT British 3rd Infantry Division

SWORD BEACH 06 JUNE 1944 UP TO 12.00 HOURS

LORD LOVAT

Known as Shimi to his friends, Lovat came from a Highland family with a stormy past – an ancestor was the last peer beheaded for treason. He joined the Commandos in 1940, and led 4 Commando on the Dieppe raid, capturing a coastal battery. On D-Day he was accompanied ashore on Sword Beach by his piper, Bill Millin, and carried a hunting rifle. He was later severely wounded, and after the war acted as Churchill's emissary to Stalin before becoming a noted cattle breeder.

south of the same village. This took longer than had been expected, largely because Hillman, which had not been bombed or shelled, was too serious an obstacle for the Suffolks to take, save by a formal attack with proper armoured support. As long as Hillman remained in German hands, it acted like a cork in the bottle.

The next brigade to land, 185th, had been ordered to capture Caen, with the infantry of 2nd King's Shropshire Light Infantry riding on tanks of the Staffordshire Yeomanry to spearhead the advance. However, the narrowness of the front and congestion on and behind the beach caused delay, and although the leading

BELOW: The scene on Queen White sector of Sword Beach at about 8.30 a.m. on D-Day. Sappers of 84th Field Company Royal Engineers are in the foreground. In the background are men of 1st Battalion, the Suffolk Regiment and Lord Lovat's commandos.

Sapper Fred Sadler

Sapper Cyril Hawkins

Sapper Jimmy Leask

elements of the brigade eventually reached the northern edge of Lebisey Wood, just three miles short of Caen, they were unable to get further. When 9th Brigade arrived, after further delay, Major General Rennie ordered it to defend the Orne bridges against attack from the west. His concern was understandable, for he had already heard that 21st Panzer Division had begun its counter-attack.

21st Panzer had been re-raised to replace the original division, lost in North Africa. Its commander lacked relevant experience: on the dawn of the invasion it was inconveniently close to the Orne and the Caen Canal, and it took time for a decision to attack west of the water obstacles. Colonel von Oppeln-Bronikowski's battle group was launched northwards, but was sharply engaged by tanks and anti-tank guns, well posted on the Perières ridge, west of Hillman, and though it just reached the coast between the 3rd British Division and the 3rd Canadian Division, it achieved little. Although 3rd Division had shrugged off the only major D-Day counter-attack, it had failed to take Caen. With the benefit of hindsight it seems that the plan was too ambitious given the proximity of German armour and the need to squeeze all attacking brigades, one by one, across the same beach.

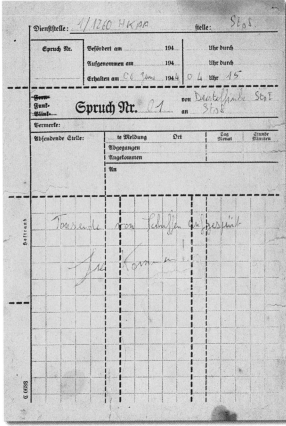

ABOVE: Terse German radio signal log timed at 4.15 am on D-Day which reads "Thousands of ships tracked. They're coming".

LEFT: Infantry advance with a Duplex Drive Sherman of 13th/18th Hussars just outside Ouistreham.

OPPOSITE: Letter from General Montgomery to his friend Major General Frank Simpson, director of military operations at the War Office, summarizing the overall situation on D+2. Montgomery wrote the letter from his tactical headquarters on the day he landed in Normandy.

PHILIPPE KIEFFER

Kieffer was born in Haiti to a family originating in Alsace. A reserve officer aboard the old battleship Courbet in 1940, he immediately joined the Free French forces. Impressed by British commandos, he raised the first French commando unit. He led 177 of his men ashore on Sword Beach, and took the casino in Ouistreham and the lock gates on the canal: his commandos suffered heavy casualties and he was twice wounded. After the war he sat in the National Assembly.

SECRET

Tac 21 Army Group
8-6-44

Seen by CREERY Tank & Airborne
11 June OTAC

My dear Simbo

You may like the following news of
our battle.

1. There is no doubt that the Germans were
surprised, and we got on shore before
they had recovered. The speed, power, and
violence of the assault carried all before
it.

2. Generally, the beach obstacles presented no
difficulty; where they were troublesome it
was because of the rough weather — and
on some beaches it was pretty rough.

3. DD Tanks.
(a) Used successfully on UTAH beaches.
(b) Failed to reach the shore on OMAHA beaches
and all sank — too rough.
(c) Were not launched on 50 DIV front as it
was too rough; were landed "dry" behind
the leading flights; casualties to AVRE
sappers high as a result, and to leading
infantry.
(d) Landed "dry" on Canadian front.
(e) Used successfully on 3 DIV front.
Generally it can be said that the DD tanks

---

proved their value, and casualties were
high when they could not be used.

4. As a guess prisoners about 6000 so far.
They consist of Germans, Russians, Poles,
Japanese, and two Turks.

5. British casualties about 1000 per
assault Division.
American casualties not known.
High proportion of officer casualties, due
to sniping behind our front.
Two Inf. Bde. Comds wounded:
  Cunningham   9 Bde
  Senior   151 Bde
Good many Inf. C.O.s killed, including
HERDON, O.C. 2 Warwicks.
No general officers are casualties.

6. The Germans are fighting well; Russians,
Poles, Japanese, and Turks, run away, and
if unable to do so, surrender.

7. Our initial attack was on a wide
front, and there were gaps between
landings. The impetus of the assault
carried us some way inland and

---

many defended localities were by-passed;
these proved very troublesome later. In
one case a complete German Bn, with
artillery, was found inside 50 DIV
area; it gave some trouble but was
eventually collected in (about 500 men).
There is still one holding out — the
radar station west of DOUVRES; it is
very strong and is held by stout-hearted
Germans.

8. Sniping in back areas has been very
troublesome, as a result of para 7.
The roads have been far from safe and
we have lost several good officers.
I have been all night myself, though
I have toured the area all day.
There have been women snipers, presumably
wives of German soldiers; the Canadians
shot 4 women snipers.

9. The Germans are doing everything they
can to hold on to CAEN. I have
decided not to have a lot of casualties
by battering up against the place; so

4

I have ordered Second Army to keep
up a good pressure at CAEN, and
to make its main effort towards
VILLERS BOCAGE and EVRECY and
thence S.E. towards FALAISE.

10. First US Army had a very sticky party
at OMAHA; and its progress at UTAH
has not been rapid.
I have therefore ordered it to join up
its two lodgement areas and to
secure CARENTAN and ISIGNY. It
will then thrust towards LA HAYE
DU PUITS and cut off the Cherbourg
peninsula.

11. The two armies have now joined
hands east of BAYEUX.

No time for more.

Yrs. ever
B. L. Montgomery.

P.T.O.

SWORD BEACH

MONDAY 12 JUNE – THURSDAY 15 JUNE
VILLERS-BOCAGE

Despite bloody Omaha and the British failure to take Caen, D-Day was a triumph: by its close over 130,000 Allied soldiers had been landed.

Over the next few days the Allies consolidated their position. First contact between British and Americans was made on 7 June, and on the 9th American troops from Utah and Omaha met. The Allies now had a continuous beachhead, although it took more fighting to secure the Carentan area and make the link between the two US corps really secure.

Having failed to take Caen early, Montgomery ordered XXX Corps to attack through Villers-Bocage and Noyers, cross the River Odon, and then push south and south-east of Tilly-sur-Seulles, outflanking Caen. Major General G. W. E. J. Erskine's 7th Armoured

> ## "[The Tiger] immediately knocked out Colonel Arthur's tank, and that of the regimental second in command, Major Carr, whom he seriously wounded, followed by the Regimental Sergeant Major's tank. Captain Dyas in the fourth tank, reversed and backed into the front garden of a nearby house."
>
> Major W. H. J. Sale, 4th County of London Yeomanry

7TH ARMOURED DIVISION

This originated as the Mobile Division, formed in Egypt in 1938, and fought throughout the desert campaign, moving on to Italy before being recalled for the invasion of Europe. The division, with its extensive experience in the Mediterranean, and a measure of war-weariness, initially found the new conditions of Normandy trying, and its commander, Major General G. W. E. J. Erskine (above) was replaced. However, the division rose above the summer's misfortunes, and it took the surrender of Hamburg and participated in the 1945 Berlin victory parade. Its jerboa badge and nickname "Desert Rats" have been inherited by the modern 7th Armoured Brigade.

PREVIOUS PAGE: German tanks moving up the battle area were repeatedly harried from the air. This photograph of Lancaster heavy bombers in action shows what the original caption calls a "really good concentration of bomb bursts" on German armour at Villers-Bocage.

LEFT: German tanks, heavily camouflaged and well spaced out to minimize the risk of air attack, moving up near Villers-Bocage.

BELOW: British 7th Armoured Division

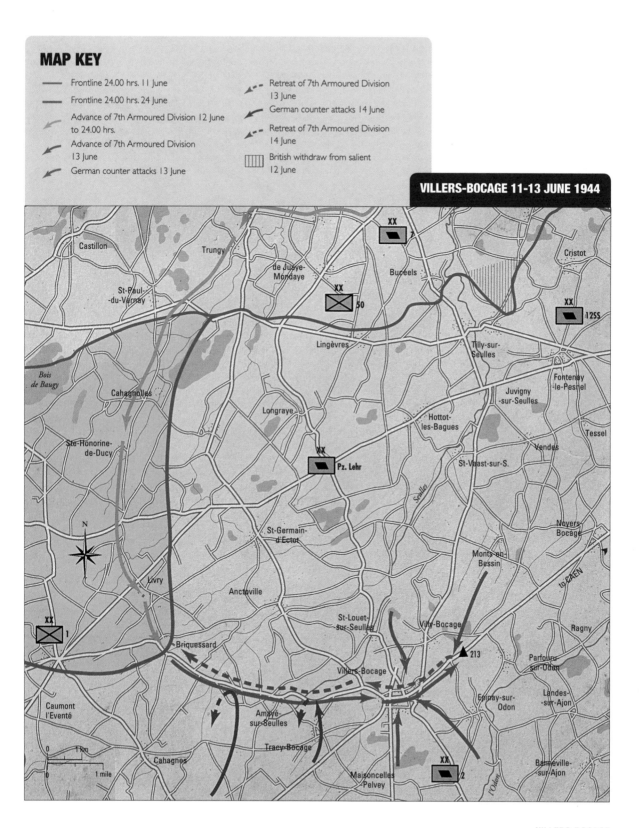

MAP KEY

— Frontline 24.00 hrs. 11 June

— Frontline 24.00 hrs. 24 June

Advance of 7th Armoured Division 12 June to 24.00 hrs.

Advance of 7th Armoured Division 13 June

German counter attacks 13 June

Retreat of 7th Armoured Division 13 June

German counter attacks 14 June

Retreat of 7th Armoured Division 14 June

British withdraw from salient 12 June

VILLERS-BOCAGE 11-13 JUNE 1944

Castillon

Trungy

de Juaye-Mondaye

Bucéels

Cristot

XX 7

St-Paul--du-Vernay

XX 50

Lingèvres

Tilly-sur-Seulles

XX 12SS

Bois de Baugy

Cahagnolles

Longraye

Hottot-les-Bagues

Juvigny-sur-Seulles

Fontenay-le-Pesnel

Ste-Honorine-de-Ducy

XX Pz. Lehr

St-Vaast-sur-S.

Vendes

Tessel

St-Germain-d'Ectot

Seulles

Noyers-Bocage

N

Livry

Anctoville

St-Louet-sur-Seulles

Monts-en-Bessin

Villy-Bocage

to CAEN

Ragny

XX 1

Briquessard

▲ 213

Parfouru-sur-Odon

Villers-Bocage

Epinay-sur-Odon

Landes--sur-Ajon

Caumont l'Eventé

Amayé-sur-Seulles

l'Odon

XX 2

Banneville-sur-Ajon

0 1 km

0 1 mile

Cahagnes

Tracy-Bocage

Maisoncelles-Pelvey

MICHAEL WITTMANN

Wittman was one of the war's most outstanding tank commanders. Between March 1943 and January 1944 his Tiger of 1st SS Panzer Division destroyed over a hundred Soviet tanks and assault guns. Transferred to Normandy in command of an SS heavy tank company, he distinguished himself at Villers-Bocage, adding swords and oak leaves to his Knight's Cross. On 8 August, during Operation Totalize, his tank was knocked out by a Sherman of the 1st Northamptonshire Yeomanry with no survivors.

Division was to lead, with 22nd Armoured Brigade at its head. On 10 June the advance began, but the bocage of little fields bounded by thick hedges was easier to defend than attack. Infantry from 56th Infantry Brigade, borrowed from 50th Division, came up that night, and the advance was resumed with infantry on hand to help with close-quarter fighting, but progress was again poor.

On 12 June 7th Armoured tried again, this time with its own infantry of 131st Brigade to help. It had crossed the River Aure and swung south so that at nightfall on the 11th its leading elements were only two miles from Caumont and five from Villers-Bocage, which was taken without difficulty on the 12th. But as the leading elements of 4th County of London Yeomanry with infantry of the Rifle Brigade moved out along the Caen road, they were assailed by a tank company commanded by SS Captain Michael Wittmann; he knocked out 12 tanks, 13 troop carriers and two anti-tank guns. Although his own tank was destroyed, he and his crew escaped. As the counter-attack gained momentum, Major General Erskine decided, with his corps commander's approval, to pull back to Tracy-Bocage, and then fell back on Livery. The action, termed "disappointing" by the British official history, was eventually to contribute to both divisional and corps commanders losing their jobs.

LEFT: A knocked-out Cromwell tank of 4th County of London Yeomanry in the main street of Villers-Bocage.

BELOW: The Tiger tank with its 88mm gun. Although it was slower than the Sherman, and less mechanically reliable, its thick armour and fearsome fire power made it a formidable defensive weapon in Normandy. The Allies reckoned that on average it cost them three tanks to knock out one Tiger.

PLUTO & MULBERRY

The Allies had a huge logistic appetite: indeed, from 15 to 19 June they landed a daily average of almost 35,000 men, 25,000 tons of stores, and 5,894 vehicles.

It was evident that the Germans would fight hard to retain Cherbourg, the only major port in the area. When its commander surrendered on 26 June, the docks had already been smashed. But a shortfall in port capacity had long been identified, and in 1941 a War Office port engineering branch was formed under Major (later Brigadier Sir Bruce) White. The Admiralty contributed through the Department of Miscellaneous Weapons Development and the Department of Naval Constructors, and US engineers also became involved. Both Churchill and Admiral Lord Louis Mountbatten, first director of Combined Operations, acted as the project's "godfathers". Dieppe lent urgency, by suggesting that the Allies would not capture a port intact.

In September 1943 instructions were issued for the construction of two harbours, Mulberry A for the Americans and Mulberry B for the British. They were to be made in Britain, towed across the

ABOVE: The floating roadway of the British Mulberry at Arromanches, photographed on 14 June, its third day of operation.

MULBERRIES IN USE: 12 JUNE– 28 NOVEMBER 1944

Personnel Landed:	231,315
Vehicles Landed:	45,181
Tons of Stores Landed:	628,000

ABOVE: A shore terminal for Tombola, which enabled tankers to pipe fuel ashore. Many of the US troops of the Petroleum Distribution Group had been oil workers in civilian life.

BELOW: One of the gigantic spools, codenamed "Conundrums", which unrolled Pluto, the cross-Channel pipeline.

Channel, and were to handle 12,000 tons of stores a day, about one-third of the total requirement. Concrete caissons (Phoenix) formed the harbour wall. They would be sheltered by breakwaters (Gooseberries) consisting of blockships and floating bombardons (Corncobs) and connected to the shore by floating roadways (Whales). The first blockships, old vessels sailing under their own steam, were sunk on 7 June. One of the stores piers of Mulberry B took loads from coasters into trucks on 14 June, and the first tank landed at Mulberry A two days later.

On 18 June the weather turned very ugly, and did not improve till the 22nd. Mulberry A was crippled and Mulberry B damaged, but was soon brought back into service. The Americans succeeded in landing stores over open beaches or into small ports, and although the piers and roadway of Mulberry A had disappeared the Gooseberries still proved invaluable. By the end of October about 25 per cent of stores, 20 per cent of personnel and 15 per cent of vehicles had been landed through Mulberry. The

development of the DUKW, essentially an amphibious truck, probably made the floating roadways redundant, but this would not have been obvious in 1943.

As early as November 1939 it had been suggested that petrol could be supplied to the continent by undersea pipe, and Pluto (Pipeline Under the Ocean) was the child of discussions between the Chief of Combined Operations and the Petroleum Warfare Department in 1942. Two pipes ran from Sandown, Isle of Wight, to terminals (one British and one American) near Port-en-Bessin, and another later ran from Dungeness to a terminal near Boulogne. The Normandy Pluto did not become operational till the end of July; until then the Allies received fuel via Tombola, buoyed pipelines connected to tankers moored offshore, which in theory (but seldom in practice) delivered 8,000 tons a day.

BELOW: Storm damage sustained by one of the piers at Mulberry A. The American harbour was ruined by the storm, and supply briefly faltered.

CHAPTER 1 - GENERAL INSTRUCTIONS.

101.   Operation NEPTUNE is the beginning of the Second Front, and entails landing U.S. and British armies in NORTHERN FRANCE.

102.   In order to supply these armies once they are landed it is necessary to have harbours for ships to unload.   Harbours that are captured will probably have been rendered unusable by the enemy so it is intended to build two artificial ones, one in the U.S. sector and one in the British sector;   these will be called MULBERRIES A and B respectively.

103.   The MULBERRIES will consist of:-

   (a)   GOOSEBERRIES, which consist of breakwaters formed by blockships (CORNCOBS) who will steam to the far shore and will be sunk early in the operation to form a breakwater,

   (b)   PHOENIX units, which will be towed across and sunk as additional breakwaters,

   (c)   BOMBARDON units, which will be towed across and moored to form an outer floating breakwater,

   (d)   WHALE units, which will be towed across to form piers for unloading inside the harbour.

Units.

104.   PHOENIX.   Large concrete caissons 200 ft. long.   There are six sizes which vary from about 6,000 tons to 2,000 tons.   Maximum draft 20 ft.

BOMBARDON.   Floating steel structures 200 ft. long and drawing 19 ft.   Units about 1,000 tons.

WHALE.   A large number of different types of units which will form the pier roadway and pierheads.   Maximum 2,000 tons.   Up to six of these pieces may be joined together to form one WHALE tow.

RIGHT: A page from the 27 May 1944 handbook for tug boats used in the cross-Channel transportation of the Mulberry Harbours.

10, Downing Street,
Whitehall.

PIERS FOR USE ON BEACHES

<u>C.C.O.</u> or deputy.

They must float up and down with the tide. The anchor problem must be mastered. Let me have the best solution worked out. Don't argue the matter. The difficulties will argue for themselves.

30. 5. 42.

ABOVE: Letter dated 30 May 1942, from Winston Churchill to the Chief of Combined Operations pressing for solutions to the initial Mulberry Harbour design problems.

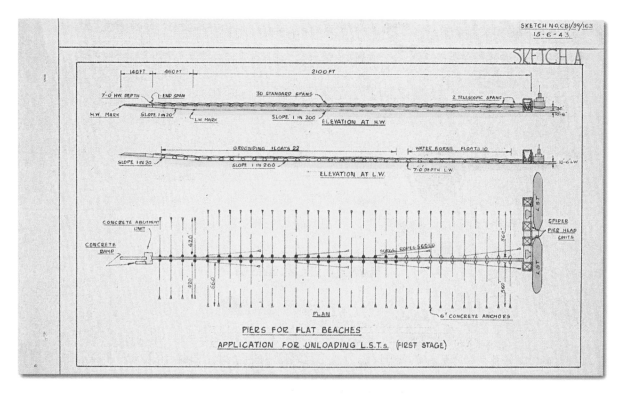

SKETCH A

PIERS FOR FLAT BEACHES

APPLICATION FOR UNLOADING L.S.T.s. (FIRST STAGE)

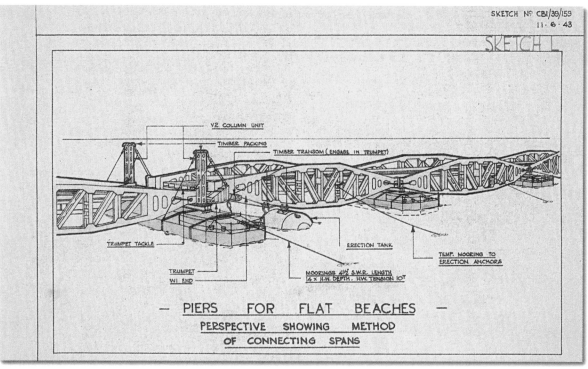

SKETCH I

— PIERS FOR FLAT BEACHES —

PERSPECTIVE SHOWING METHOD

OF CONNECTING SPANS

LEFT: Early concept drawings for the Mulberry Piers, produced mid-June 1943 in response to Churchill's letter.

RIGHT: Churchill visited Normandy soon after D-Day. This photograph shows his evident satisfaction in an invention he had done so much to support.

BELOW: Mulberry B at work. An outer line of caissons provided shelter from the waves and enabled some vessels to be unloaded into DUKWs, while vehicles could be landed on the floating pierheads and driven ashore along the piers.

OPERATION EPSOM

The great storm came at a bad moment for the Allies, for both were preparing offensives: the Americans into the Cotentin, heading for Cherbourg, and further south, towards St-Lô, while the British were gearing up for another attempt to take Caen.

Despite the damage sustained by the Mulberries, the Gooseberries, which had been inserted off the other invasion beaches, did rather better, though that at Utah was damaged. However, the storm reduced the pace of Allied build-up, and enabled the Germans to shift extra forces into Normandy to buttress their front.

The next British attack was to consist of a minor attack east of the Orne, in which 152nd Brigade of 51st Highland Division was to capture the village of Ste-Honorine-de-la-Chardonnerette, just south of 6th Airborne Division's old dropping zones. The storm delayed the attack until 23 June but it proved successful, and the village was secured by midday. An altogether larger venture was Operation Epsom, on the other side of Caen, which was to involve part of both the bruised XXX Corps and the newly arrived but still incomplete VIII Corps under Lieutenant General Sir Richard O'Connor. There were over 700 guns available to support the attack, and three cruisers and the monitor HMS Roberts were also to assist. The main blow was to fall between Tilly-sur-Seulles in the west and Carpiquet, not far from Caen, in the east.

ABOVE TOP: Infantrymen of 6th Battalion, Royal Scots Fusiliers, part of the 15th (Scottish) Division, on 26 June 1944, ready to advance under a lowering sky.

ABOVE: Royal Scots Fusiliers walk forward into the mist on the first day of Epsom.

ABOVE: British 49th Infantry Division

RICHARD O'CONNOR

O'Conner was commissioned into the Cameronians in 1909 and was a temporary lieutenant colonel in 1918. He made his reputation commanding the British attack into the Western Desert in December 1941, but was unluckily captured soon afterwards. Escaping from captivity after the Italian surrender in 1943, he was a corps commander in Normandy, but never really regained his old touch for armoured warfare. Adjutant general of the army after the war, he resigned on a point of principle in 1947.

On 25 June 49th Division of XXX Corps, fighting its first battle, attacked Juvigny, Vendes and Rauray in an effort to secure the eastern shoulder of the attack sector, and though it made some progress it failed to take the Rauray spur, which caused repeated trouble over the next few days. The following morning, in weather so bad that flying was out of the question and cross-country going poor, VIII Corps struck out for the Odon but did not quite reach it, though a bridge was seized intact the next day by 15th (Scottish) Division. The Scots were supported by the tanks of 11th Armoured Division and 31st Tank Brigade, in a bitter battle with attacks meeting stern resistance and repeated counter-attacks. By nightfall on the 28th there was a salient five miles deep but only two wide into the German lines, and it had attracted most of the German armoured reserves. A series of counter-attacks, which peaked on 1 July, were beaten off, and the battle ended with the British secure across the Odon south-west of Caen, but still without sufficient leverage to wrest that city from the Germans. In one sense Epsom had failed, and had cost 15th Division alone 2,500 casualties. But it had blunted the cutting edge of German armour so badly that there was no longer any chance of it mounting a comprehensive counter-attack on the Allied bridgehead.

ABOVE: 15th Scottish Infantry Division

ABOVE: British 11th Armoured Division

RIGHT: Infantrymen, on the lookout for snipers, approach a breached wall in the village of St-Manvieu on the left of 15th (Scottish) Division's attack.

PAUL HAUSSER

Hausser had a conventional army career, retiring as a major general in 1932, but joining the SS two years later. Badly wounded as a divisional commander on the Eastern Front, he commanded 2nd SS Panzer Corps in June 1944, and counter-attacked Operation Epsom. However, his plan fell into Allied hands and the attack failed. He took command of 7th Army on 29 June. Hausser escaped from the Falaise pocket and, an SS colonel general, commanded an army group until dismissed in 1945.

MAP KEY

—— Frontline 24 June

—— Frontline 25 June

—— Frontline 26 June

—— Frontline 30 June

OPERATION EPSOM 24-30 JUNE 1944

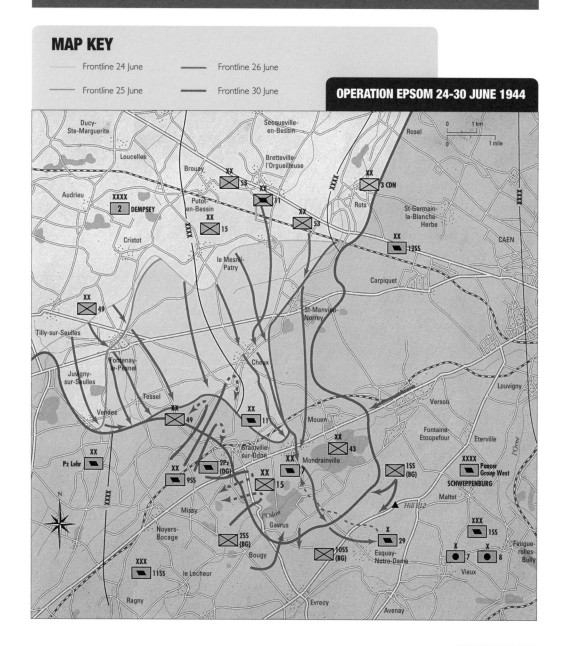

BOCAGE FIGHTING & CHERBOURG

The terrain of Normandy presented sharp contrasts. The area around Caen and Falaise was open, with big fields whose wheat stood almost shoulder high.

Further west the ground grew more enclosed. The Bessin, around Bayeux, was noted for lush pastures and apple orchards: apples and cream still define cooking à la Normande. John Ruskin declared in 1848 that the Cotentin resembled Worcestershire but was even more beautiful. To its south, around St-Lô, came Norman bocage in its most extreme form, a chequerboard of little fields, stout hedges on high banks, and sunken lanes which reminded visitors of Devon or Dorset.

The advance on Cherbourg through the Cotentin was comparatively straightforward, and Lieutenant General "Lighting Joe" Collins of the US VII Corps defined it, just after the great storm, as "the major effort of the American army". The attack began in earnest on 22 June, with 9th and 79th Divisions moving against the city after heavy air attack, while 4th Division sealed it off from the east. The Germans fought well, their commander, Lieutenant General Karl-Wilhelm von Schlieben, enjoined by Hitler to "defend the last bunker and leave to the enemy not a harbour but a field

of ruins". Three days later Schlieben told Rommel that the city's fall was inevitable and "further sacrifices cannot alter anything," but was again ordered to "fight to the last cartridge ...". The powerful Fort du Roule fell that day, and Schlieben himself was captured on the

ABOVE: An American infantryman dashes across a street whose German sign proclaims it the Cherbourg West Diversion.

ABOVE: US 79th Infantry Division

ABOVE: US 9th Infantry Division

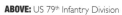

JOE COLLINS

Commissioned into the infantry in 1917, Collins was commanding a division in Hawaii when war broke out in 1941. His tough style gained him the nickname "Lightning Joe", and he was selected to command VII Corps in the invasion of Europe. In 1944 he came to notice as conqueror of Cherbourg, and was photographed with his defeated opponent Lieutenant General Karl-Wilhelm von Schlieben, commander of 709th Infantry Division and the Cherbourg garrison.

26th, though he refused to surrender his command, and sporadic fighting flickered on a little longer.

Although Hitler ordered Rundstedt to consider a large armoured counter-attack, the opening of Operation Epsom drew German reserves to the east, and Hitler concluded that, for the moment, he would have to fight "a war of attrition" to confine the Allies to their beachhead. This was significantly smaller than planners had hoped, leading to problems in getting the right balance of combat and support troops into the lodgement area, and reducing the

BELOW: Although billed as a combat shot of the advance on Cherbourg, the photograph's careful composition suggests a measure of posing.

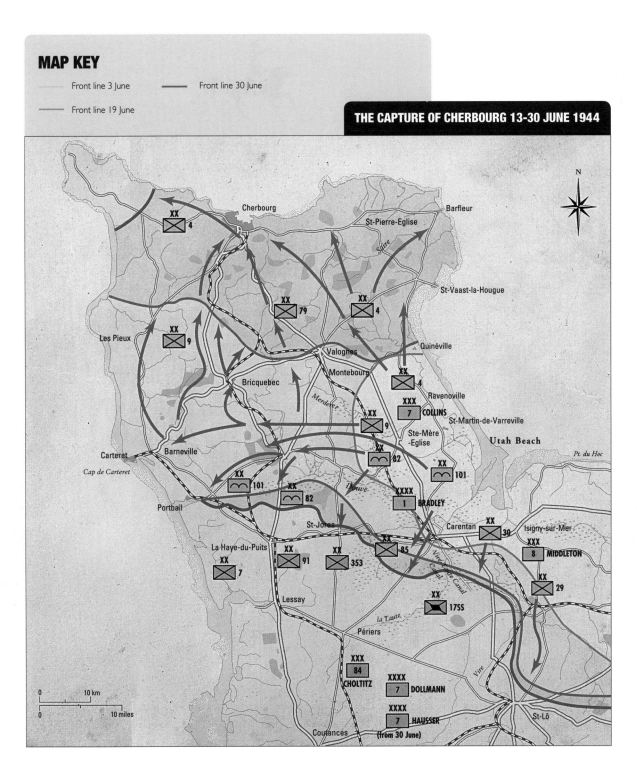

THE CAPTURE OF CHERBOURG 13–30 JUNE 1944

N

Cherbourg

Barfleur

St-Pierre-Eglise

XX 4

Séire

St-Vaast-la-Hougue

XX 79

Les Pieux

XX 9

XX 4

Quinéville

Valognes

Montebourg

Bricquebec

XX 4

Ravenoville

Merderet

XXX 7 COLLINS

St-Martin-de-Varreville

XX 9

Ste-Mère-Eglise

Carteret

Barneville

XX 82

Cap de Carteret

XX 101

Utah Beach

Pt. du Hoc

XX 101

Douve

XX 82

XXXX 1 BRADLEY

Portbail

St-Jores

Carentan

XX 30

Isigny-sur-Mer

XX 85

Vire-Taute Canal

XXX 8 MIDDLETON

La Haye-du-Puits

XX 7

XX 91

XX 353

Canal

XX 29

Lessay

XX 17SS

la Taute

Périers

Vire

XXX 84 CHOLTITZ

XXXX 7 DOLLMANN

XXXX 7 HAUSSER

(from 30 June)

Coutances

St-Lô

0   10 km

0   10 miles

programme of airfield construction, notably on the open country around Caen.

Bradley's First US Army began its thrust south at the beginning of July. Reports that the fall of Cherbourg had led to a sharp diminution in German fighting power soon proved incorrect as the advance ran into determined defenders strongly posted in difficult country. US casualties were heavy: 325th Glider Infantry Regiment of 82nd Airborne, with an establishment of 135 officers and 2,838 men, had 55 officers and 1,245 men on 2 July but 41 officers and 956 men four days later: its strongest rifle company had 57 men, its weakest just 12. Junior leadership was at a premium: in 359th Infantry one company and two leaderless platoons of another were commanded by Private Barney H. Prosser. It was clear that there would be no easy ride through the bocage.

RIGHT: Coder-decoder machine used by US troops in the field to send and receive coded messages.

OPPOSITE Happy warriors? Defenders of Cherbourg march past a statue of Napoleon on their way to prisoner of war cages. The censor has obliterated background detail which would have revealed how badly damaged the docks were.

BELOW: Major General Collins talking to an American captain at Fort du Roule, one of the last German defences to fall before the capture of Cherbourg.

OPERATION CHARNWOOD

At the beginning of July, Caen still denied Montgomery room for manoeuvre on the eastern flank of the battlefield.

The Canadians captured Carpiquet and its airfield from their old enemies, 12th SS Panzer Division, on 4 July, and on the night of the 7th 450 Lancasters and Halifaxes of RAF Bomber Command, used for the first time in direct support of ground forces, struck Caen itself. The city had already been badly damaged by bombing and by shelling from land and sea – a shell from HMS *Rodney* had felled the fine Gothic spire of the church of St-Pierre – and the preparations for the final Allied assault put the last dreadful touches to its martyrdom. One of the British soldiers who entered the city on 9 July thought it "just a waste of brick and stone, like a field of corn that has been ploughed".

The attack on Caen was carried out by I Corps. While 59th and 3rd Divisions attacked from the north, 3rd Canadian Division struck south-eastwards. The British official history acknowledges that, while the Germans used snipers and mortars to contest the advance through the city, "these gave little trouble compared with the bomb craters, the rubble and the large blocks of locally quarried stone which choked the narrow streets." The attacking corps lost about 3,500 men, and of its opponents, the infantry of 12th SS Panzer Division was reduced to battalion strength and 16th Luftwaffe Field Division had lost three-quarters of its men.

PREVIOUS PAGE: Repeated bombing did terrible damage to the ancient city of Caen. This RAF photograph was taken in the first week of the Normandy campaign.

BELOW: A Bren-gunner and riflemen in the ruins, amongst blocks of the locally quarried pierre de Caen.

> "The tommy attacks with great masses of infantry and many tanks. We fight as long as possible, but by the time the survivors try to pull back, we realize that we are surrounded."
>
> Private Zimmer, 12th SS Panzer Division

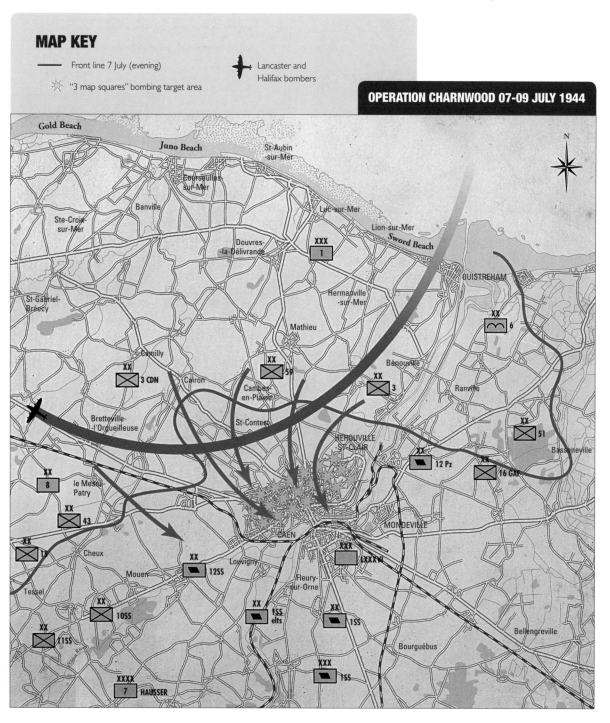

MAP KEY

— Front line 7 July (evening)

※ "3 map squares" bombing target area

✈ Lancaster and Halifax bombers

OPERATION CHARNWOOD 07-09 JULY 1944

When you left your wife

you tried to console her in the belief, that by «this very last, great effort of all Allies together»

the war will definitely be over within a few months.

Well - in between perhaps you already changed your mind a bit, getting just the first, slight impression of what means

Invasion

In order to preserve you from any further disappointments You ought to know:

You are facing German soldiers now, defending the forefield of their home.

S W 5

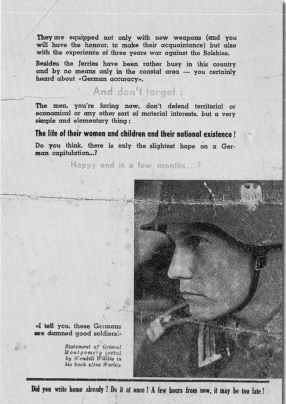

They are equipped not only with new weapons (and you will have the honour, to make their acquaintance) but also with the experience of three years war against the Bolshies.

Besides the Jerries have been rather busy in this country and by no means only in the coastal area — you certainly heard about «German accuracy».

And don't forget :

The men, you're facing now, don't defend territorial or economical or any other sort of material interests, but a very simple and elementary thing :

The life of their women and children and their national existence !

Do you think, there is only the slightest hope on a German capitulation...?

Happy end in a few months...?

«I tell you, these Germans are damned good soldiers!»

Statement of General Montgomery quoted by Wendell Willkie in his book «One World»

Did you write home already ? Do it at once ! A few hours from now, it may be too late !

ABOVE: British 59th Infantry Division

ABOVE: A propaganda leaflet dropped on Allied troops in Normandy by the Luftwaffe.

RIGHT: A section of Royal Engineers moving into Caen to deal with booby traps and unexploded bombs.

With Caen at last secured, the British mounted a limited operation to widen the bridgehead over the Odon created by Operation Epsom. 43rd Wessex Division, supported by two tank brigades and a Highland infantry brigade and abundant artillery, struck out at Hill 112 in an attack that produced "a battle of shattering intensity even by the standards of Normandy" and cost the British 2,000 casualties. By its end the men from those county regiments, which rarely caught the headlines but always formed the solid weight of the British army, held half the hill, and its long, low crest now bears their memorial.

LIFTS WITH BELTS OR WEBBING

1. TWO BELTS. Tie two belts, or webbing, together in a ring. Slip one loop under his arms. Put your head through the other (fig. 9).

2. THREE BELTS. Join three belts together. One loop under his buttocks, the other under his arms. If he can sit, lift him like a haversack. Your hands are free to use a rifle (fig. 10).

3. IF HE CAN'T SIT UP. Lie on your back on top of him. Put your arms through the loops. Roll over. Get up.

FIRST AID FOR FIGHTING MEN

Your life and those of your comrades may depend upon your having this folder always at hand.

FIRST AID FOR FIGHTING MEN

CHARLES KEOGH, F.R.C.S.

This folder is for the Fighting Man, to help him to go on fighting, and to aid his Friend in that cold interval between getting hit and getting help

Printed and Published by
SIFTON, PRAED & CO., LTD.
ST. JAMES'S STREET, S.W. 1.

Revised Edition

---

1. FIRST AID IS COMMON SENSE plus a little specialised knowledge. First Aid saves lives and stops panic.

2. A LIGHTLY WOUNDED MAN, if given First Aid, can go on fighting. Act quickly.

3. A BADLY WOUNDED MAN looks pale and sweaty. Be prepared for this. Treat him like a child. Calm him. Calm the men in your post. This is First Aid.

4. WOUNDS CAN LOOK FRIGHTFUL. Be prepared for this. Remember modern Surgeons can do wonders. Nature does her best to heal all wounds. But give Nature a chance. Stop wounds getting worse. That is your job. That is First Aid.

5. DON'T DISTURB A WOUNDED MAN too much unless you have to. Nature will tell him how to lie in the safest and most comfortable position.

6. LOOK, THINK AND THEN ACT. There may be three men wounded at once. Treat the most urgent first. Keep under cover. If mechanised, turn off petrol. Look out for falling walls. Any fool can be brave and get killed; be brave and don't get killed, and save your friend instead. Look, think, and then act.

7. STOP BLEEDING. A man bleeds to death very quickly. Stop it with your hands. There is no time to wash. Put your fist into the wound. Hold it there. This gives you time. Stuff in a piece of cloth or field dressing. Tie a bandage over it tight. Use another field dressing or strips of cloth for this. Anything will do - but be quick (fig. 1).

8. IF YOU CAN'T STOP IT that way, slip a piece of string round the leg or arm higher up. A pull-through or sling will do, tie it over his uniform. Tie one knot (fig. 2). Put a pencil or piece of wood on the knot (fig. 3). Tie twice over the stick. Tie a reef knot. Tie any knot if you don't know how (figs. 4 & 5). Twist the stick until the bleeding stops. Keep it in position by tying the ends down. This is a Tourniquet.

9. A TOURNIQUET can save a life and a limb. It can also kill a limb. Loosen a tourniquet every quarter of an hour. Four times an hour. If you don't, the limb will die. So don't put one on unless you have to.

10. IN WAR, a wounded man may be hours or days before he gets to a Surgeon. If ever you put on a tourniquet, put a label on. Write "Tourniquet applied 9 a.m. Tuesday. Loosen four times an hour. Tighten again if bleeding starts." Fix the label where it can be seen.

11. BROKEN BONES. Place the limb in its most natural position and you can't go wrong. Don't let a broken limb flap. Sharp ends of broken bone can cut arteries and nerves to pieces. Tie a broken arm to the chest with

any kind of bandage. But tie it firmly (fig. 6). Tie a broken leg to the other leg. Use as many bandages as possible. Foot to foot, knee to knee, thigh to thigh (fig. 7).

12. SMALL PUNCTURED WOUNDS are often more dangerous than dreadful bloody ones. A spent bullet from the air can go right through a man. Punctured wounds must be seen by a Doctor.

13. CHEST, HEAD, AND BODY WOUNDS. Cover them. Stop the bleeding as best you can. They look much worse than they are.

14. CARRYING A WOUNDED MAN under fire. Keep under cover. Tie his wrists together. Crawl on hands and knees on top of him. Put your neck under his wrists, and drag him along underneath you. You can go a long way like this, and won't give away the position of your post to the enemy (fig. 8).

15. WHEN TO GIVE A MAN A DRINK. Give any wounded man a drink of anything you have - but do not give a drink to a man with a wound in the belly, or to a man who cannot swallow. You will kill them if you do. Remember, no drink to those two men. But you can moisten the lips.

16. SHOCK. Shock kills more men than bullets. Shock is a mixture of pain, fear and cold. Do what you can to stop all three. Shock kills brave men.

17. BURNS. Cover burns. You can do no more. Wrap him round in blankets. Keep him warm.

18. PHOSPHORUS BURNS. Hold it under water. Wipe off phosphorus. Keep it wet.

19. GAS. Gas on skin. Wipe it off quickly. Rub in gas ointment. Quick action stops nasty burns. Gas in eyes. Bathe quickly in clean water. Quick action stops blindness. Gas in lungs. Keep him warm. Carry him back. Do not let him walk.

20. KEEP YOUR FEET CLEAN. Keep your underclothes and socks clean. Dirty wounds fester.

21. WHEN A MAN GETS HIT BESIDE YOU. a. Calm yourself. b. Stop his bleeding. c. Keep him warm.

22. THAT IS ALL YOU NEED TO KNOW. Courage in disaster. Courage in the presence of a wounded man. First Aid can save a situation and save a friend.

CHARLES KEOGH, F.R.C.S.,
London Hospital

ABOVE: First-aid instruction leaflet issued to British troops in Normandy to help them deal with battle casualties before the arrival of trained medics.

LEFT: A British sniper in Caen. Despite his camouflaged helmet and firing position, he is running a risk by being so close to the open window.

ABOVE: A British soldier gives a helping hand to an old lady amid the utter desolation of Caen. One soldier wrote of the inhabitants that "one could hardly look them in the face, knowing who had done this".

MEDICS

Wounds and death are the currency of war, and both sides paid dearly as the fighting hardened into attrition.

By the end of June the British and Canadians had lost 24,698 killed, wounded and missing, and the Americans 37,034, a total of 61,732 Allied casualties. At the end of August these figures were 83,825 and 125,847, 209,672 in total. The dead were often buried near where they fell, with chaplains saying a few words over their graves and carefully recording the sites. The burial grounds we now see, whatever their nationality, are largely "concentration" cemeteries, the bodies beneath their greensward having been moved to new resting-places after the tide of war had ebbed away.

ABOVE: Air evacuation was widely used in Normandy. Here a patient is lifted from an ambulance into a C-47 transport aircraft for the flight to England.

RIGHT: A US Army nurse takes the blood pressure reading of a soldier suffering from burns. Allied use of female nurses in Normandy gave a fillip to morale. Montgomery opined that: "No man can nurse like a woman, though many think they can."

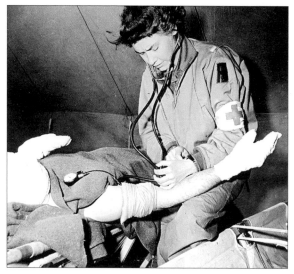

Wounded soldiers received aid from comrades or a company medic – all armies had a "First Field Dressing" to staunch the flow of blood – but it was not until they reached their regimental aid post that they could expect qualified medical attention. There they might be treated and sent back to the line, prepared for evacuation to a dressing station, or made as comfortable as possible to await an inevitable death. Until hospitals could be established in France all casualties would be evacuated to Britain, but an embryo medical organization went in on D-Day. Field dressing stations gave life-saving treatment, and then sent their patients back to casualty clearing stations. General hospitals were speedily established: there were six in the British sector by the end of June. Most men wounded in action or seriously ill were evacuated, but psychiatric casualties, with what was then called "battle fatigue", were treated in France, mainly in divisional recuperation centres. However, psychiatric casualties fell as the grim struggle in the beachhead was replaced by the more open warfare of August, and most centres were closed down.

Casualties sent to Britain at first went by sea, but air evacuation began on 13 June, and by the end of August 57,426 British and Canadian casualties had been evacuated by sea and another 22,646 flown out. Several hospitals were closed in late August so that they could follow the Allied advance across France: of the remaining 29,000 beds in British and Canadian hospitals, only 15,000 were maintained and just 9,700 were occupied.

Normandy produced a casualty pattern which First World War veterans would have recognized, with shells and mortar bombs causing most injuries. However, there had been notable advances since 1918, with the development of antibiotics, new antiseptics, and blood transfusions. In 1943 penicillin was very rare: in Normandy there was sufficient to treat all Allied casualties. Overall, 21 per cent of Allied wounded were operated on in the first "golden hour" after being hit, and another 47 per cent were operated on in the next six. A wounded US soldier, for instance, was half as likely to die in the Second World War as he was in the First.

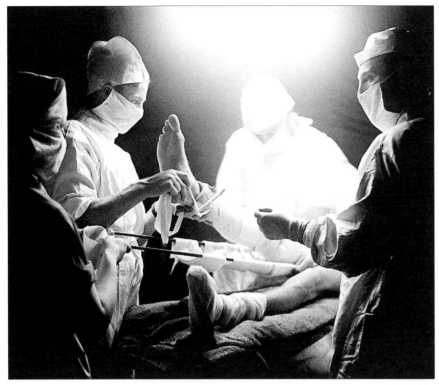

LEFT An operation in progress in the 79th General Hospital, Bayeux, on 20 June.

BELOW: Many soldiers wounded early in the fighting were evacuated on landing craft that had arrived with supplies.

OVERLEAF: June 1944 diary kept by Staff Sergeant Murray Goldman of the 3rd Medical Battalion, 505th Parachute Infantry Regiment of 82nd Airborne Division. Pages read from top to bottom from left to right.

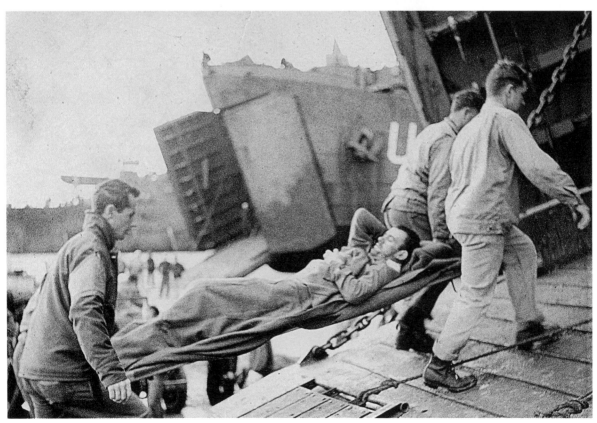

June 5 - Left Cottesmore about eleven - flew all over England then over Channel came into France at 0200 - nice and quiet + lots of smoke. Commented that this was easy. Suddenly tracer + flack - red and green. Plane started violent evasive action. Green light and went - Plane was on its side and low, about 150. terrific tracer coming up into chutes. Slipped away for all I was worth. one man screaming.

Landed easy and stayed flat - reason - grazing fire - terribly scared. Crawled into hole and took off equipment. Lots of firing - C-47's still coming - men still jumping into hell. One plane burning, but men bail out. met two jumpers + joined. met 8 more - met 20 more - feel good now - all kinds of weapons. Now we seek trouble - tore down telephone wires. No germans.

June 6 next morning

Joined a mixed group of 502 - 506 - 508 - 505 men and came to farmhouse. produced map and frenchman showed St Mere Eglise to us. Occasional sniper fire but inaccurate. Reached St mere Eglise about noon and found that Lt. H. had town taken. moved into a big building and set up hospital. Gliders had taken a hell of a beating - crashed all over countryside. Wounded pouring in now.

Companies set up town defence and prepare to hold town at all costs as ordered - already we are surrounded and fighting. Town being shelled and mortared. Eighty-eight artillery tearing hell out of us - wounded pouring in now - Hospital hit repeatedly. Germans want that town. Getting dark now - this night will be pure hell cause we are all alone + cut off. The boys are fighting like cornered lions. Even advancing. German wounded in hospital.

night

Violent enemy artillery and infiltrating attacks - some Germans enter town. They don't leave it again - they are dead. Tanks knocked out just outside of town by G.I's with grenades. Our guys are strictly mean now. They are fighting mad. Morning and we still hold town. But what a price. Hospital choked with wounded. Wounded from all over,

countryside coming in now. What a god damned mess. And still the bastard beach force does not relieve us. Hospital being shelled & hit repeatedly. Kitchen blown in. Back yard full of shell holes - no windows glass & plaster and bloody rags and wounded and dying men all over the place. Handful of aid men dog tired. Sleep - what is that?

June 7. Next Morning

Repeat performance artillery and sniper & attacks, and wounded again. No more room any place in hospital but still they come. The afternoon the 4th & Div. 8th day comes in _____ - so that we good ____ command attacks with our ____ on attacking ____ ____ infantry in our rear. Some ____ ____ guy ____ ____ _____ but ____ ____ ____ ____

Moved all wounded out with Evacuation to collecting company - packed up & moved up to join bn. again. More wounded in new area, but we have transportation now & work with system. Town is Fresville - slightly hot. To noon 8th June -

June 9 - Moved to house in Grainville - real sleep on a mattress. Some more wounded. 88mm shells ____ close. June 10 - Fairly quiet - snipers and occasional artillery - air raid at night.

BATTLE FOR ST-LÔ

The Germans had restructured their chain of command.

Field Marshal Günther von Kluge replaced Rundstedt (retired for the penultimate time) as Commander in Chief West, and on 17 July also took over Army Group B when Rommel was wounded by strafing RAF aircraft. Panzer Group West (General Heinrich Eberbach) was responsible for the British sector, and 7th Army, commanded by SS General Paul Hausser (who had replaced Colonel General Friedrich Dollmann) was facing the Americans. Hausser had two corps, LXXXIV towards the coast and II Parachute

inland. Although many of the latter's men were parachutists in name only, their robust morale, numerous automatic weapons and plentiful anti-tank Panzerfaust made them ideal for this sort of fighting.

The chief objective of Lieutenant General Omar Bradley's First US Army was the town of St-Lô, as important, in its way, to western Normandy as Caen was to the east, and which, like Caen, had

ABOVE: The perils of the bocage: an American patrol under air-burst artillery fire.

been heavily bombed. It was an important traffic centre, but had, as the US official history admits, accrued psychological value so that its retention or capture "would have a strong effect on the morale of the opposing forces". It lay in the sector attacked by XIX Corps, commanded by Major General Charles H. Corlett. The key to St-Lô was the long Martinville Ridge, crowned by Point 192, east of the city. The central part of the ridge was attacked by 29th Division of XIX Corps, while Point 192 was

MAP KEY

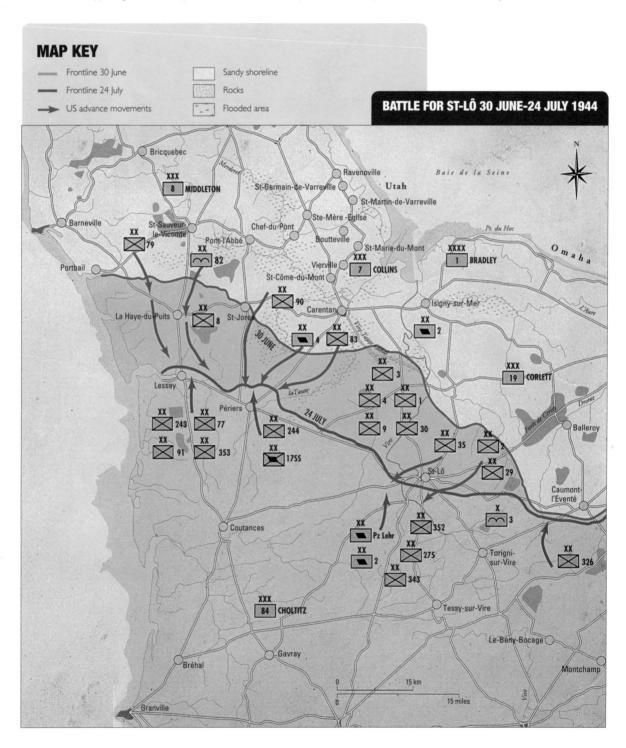

——	Frontline 30 June	▢	Sandy shoreline
——	Frontline 24 July	▨	Rocks
➔	US advance movements	▨	Flooded area

BATTLE FOR ST-LÔ 30 JUNE–24 JULY 1944

124/125

OMAR BRADLEY

Though he graduated from West Point in 1915, Bradley saw no overseas service in the First World War. In 1941 he jumped from lieutenant colonel to brigadier general, and commanded divisions before taking over II Corps. In Sicily his corps was under Patton's US Seventh Army, but when Bradley commanded US ground troops in Normandy, Patton was under his command. A competent, level-headed general, Bradley tolerated Montgomery better than many. He was later US Army Chief of Staff and chairman of the Joint Chiefs.

assailed by 2nd Division of Major General Leonard T. Gerow's V Corps.

Point 192 fell on 11 July after being hit by 45 tons of shells, and its capture enabled the Americans to look along the ridge towards XIX Corps' objective. After slow progress by 29th Division on 11–12 July, Corlett committed his reserve, the 35th Division, and on 16 July, after a bitter see-saw battle, it took Point 122, the highest point of the ridge in the corps sector. 29th Division entered St-Lô on 18 July, taking with it the flag-draped coffin of Major Thomas D. Howie, commander of 3rd Battalion 116th Infantry, whose last radio message had announced characteristically: "Will do."

LEFT: U.S 29th Infantry Division

BELOW: An American tank destroyer (a self-propelled anti-tank gun with a limited turret traverse and open top) dealing, at close range, with German positions in St-Lô.

OPERATION GOODWOOD

Montgomery was still overall ground force commander, although his days as such were numbered. The Americans would form an army group once they had sufficient troops, leaving Montgomery commanding the Anglo-Canadian 21st Army Group while Bradley stepped up to command the US 12th Army Group.

On 10 July Montgomery outlined his plan for the break-out. The Americans were to burst out of the bocage, exploiting down to Brittany and round to Le Mans and Alençon. But before this the British would mount their own offensive, Operation Goodwood. The timings for both operations slipped: it took the Americans longer than expected to secure St-Lô, and bad weather delayed Goodwood.

We cannot be certain whether Goodwood was intended to attract German armour, or was in fact a genuine attempt at a breakout. Major General "Pip" Roberts, of 11th Armoured Division, thought that Falaise

ABOVE: The impact of strategic bombers, 18 July. Some bombs were fused to explode instantaneously, leaving only small craters which would not impede the advance.

RIGHT: The Guards Armoured Division

LEFT: British tanks moving up for Operation Goodwood. Marshalling the three attacking armoured divisions, each with more than 3,000 vehicles, including almost 300 tanks, was no easy task.

was his objective, and Lieutenant General Miles Dempsey, of 2nd Army, believed it was "more than possible that the Huns will break" enabling him to exploit. Even Montgomery told the Chief of the Imperial General Staff that he hoped to "loose a corps of three armoured divisions into the open country about the Caen-Falaise road." Montgomery was subject to increasing pressure to expand the beachhead, and in particular to seize more ground for the construction of airfields. Moreover, he proposed to use heavy bombers to prepare the way for Goodwood, and knew that he would not get them save for an operation of first importance.

The plan was simple enough. Three armoured divisions, the Guards, 7th and 11th, would attack through a narrow corridor between the Orne and the Bois de Bavent, fanning out as soon as there was space, to take the Bourgebus Ridge and exploit beyond it. On the morning of 18 July more than 2,000 RAF and US bombers attacked the little villages forming a framework of defence, and 11th Armoured Division moved off on the heels of the bombing. So narrow was its corridor that it led with a single regiment – 3rd Royal Tanks – and it was not until the advance was well under way that another regiment, 2nd Fife and Forfar Yeomanry, could come up. The first line of defence, furnished by the unlucky 16th Luftwaffe Field Division, was shattered by the bombing, and serious damage had also been done to 21st Panzer Division behind it. But the defence gradually came to life. Tough-minded officers like Major Hans von Luck, who ordered an anti-aircraft battery commander, at pistol point, to take on advancing tanks, animated the defence, and SS General Sepp Dietrich, commanding 1st SS Panzer Corps, ordered up reinforcements.

The 3rd Royal Tanks were beginning to climb the ridge when they

MILES DEMPSEY

An infantry officer in the First World War, Dempsey did well as a brigadier in 1940, and Montgomery requested him as a corps commander after El Alamein. Thereafter Dempsey moved in Montgomery's wake, commanding 2nd Army from early 1944. He was easy to work with, and Bradley applauded his lack of "jealousy or anger". He made little mark as a commander, probably because he saw himself as Montgomery's loyal lieutenant. Goodwood was essentially his plan, though, and he was optimistic that it would achieve a breakthrough.

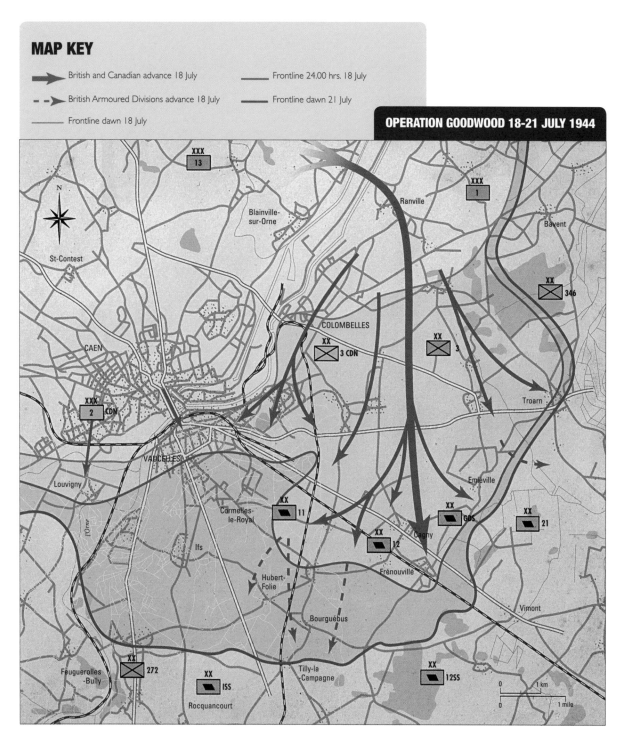

British and Canadian advance 18 July

British Armoured Divisions advance 18 July

Frontline dawn 18 July

Frontline 24.00 hrs. 18 July

Frontline dawn 21 July

OPERATION GOODWOOD 18-21 JULY 1944

N

XXX
13

XXX
1

Ranville

Blainville-
sur-Orne

Bavent

St-Contest

XX
346

COLOMBELLES

CAEN

XX
3 CDN

XX
3

Troarn

XXX
2 CDN

VAUCELLES

Louvigny

Emiéville

Cormelles-
le-Royal

XX
11

XX
GDS

XX
21

l'Orne

XX
12

Cagny

Ifs

Frénouville

Hubert-
Folie

Vimont

Bourguébus

Feuguerolles
-Bully

XX
272

XX
ISS

Tilly-la-
Campagne

XX
12SS

Rocquancourt

0   1 km

0   1 mile

were engaged by 88mm anti-tank guns, and Sherman after Sherman burst into flames. Although the British eventually secured the villages atop the ridge, any chance of a breakthrough had gone. When the battle ended on 20 July, 2nd Army had lost over 400 tanks and 6,000 men. If the tanks could be replaced from stocks in the beachhead, the loss of manpower was more serious, for this was an army scraping the bottom of its recruiting barrel. Montgomery admitted that he was over-optimistic at a press conference on the 18th, and Eisenhower was "as blue as indigo" about poor progress. Much had gone wrong in Goodwood. But one fact was undeniable: it had indeed attracted German armour to the east.

OPERATION COBRA

On 5 July Eisenhower observed that three factors were making life hard for the Americans: German fighting quality, the nature of the country, and the weather.

By the time they took St-Lô the Americans had learnt a good deal about bocage fighting, and if they were well aware of how unpleasant this was for them, they underestimated the damage that they were doing to the Germans. On 13 July Kluge, who arrived in Normandy full of enthusiasm, warned Hitler's staff that his infantry was worn perilously thin. He needed more tanks "to act as corset stays behind the troops". The situation was now "very serious. ... If a hole breaks open, I have to patch it".

Eisenhower was disappointed by Goodwood, and affirmed that he was "pinning our immediate hopes on Bradley's attack". Montgomery, meanwhile, ordered Dempsey to "fatten up" his operations in order to ensure that the Germans could not swing to meet the forthcoming attack, Operation Cobra. The original Cobra plan was modest, and envisaged an attack southwards to Coutances and then a jab westwards, to cut off the defenders of the coastal strip, and leave the US First Army consolidating on the line Coutances-Caumont, ready to exploit further. The key breakthrough was to be made by VII Corps, tightly concentrated just west of St-Lô, and before the attack German positions were to be saturated by heavy bombers. General Collins' infantry would attack after the bombing, and once they had created a gap in the defences his armoured divisions would roll on through.

ABOVE: American infantry and tank destroyers west of St-Lô.

RIGHT: US 4th Armoured Division

BELOW: A US Sherman tank with the modification to its hull. These "horns" enabled the tank to rip its way through the hedges-on-banks, so typical of the bocage.

GEORGE S. PATTON

Patton came from a well-to-do family with military traditions. Commissioned in 1909, he commanded a tank brigade in France in 1918 with great success. He led an armoured division in 1941 and was an army commander in 1943, but was shelved after slapping two shell-shocked soldiers. Patton commanded Third Army in its dash across France in 1944, but mismanaged the campaign to take Metz. Flamboyant, profane, gifted but flawed, Patton died after a car crash in 1945.

> ## "It was hell. ... The planes kept coming overhead like a conveyor belt, and the bomb carpets came down, now ahead, now on the right, now on the left. "
>
> ### Lieutenant General Fritz Bayerlein, Panzer Lehr Division

LEFT: US Third Army

BELOW FAR LEFT: An American column of jeeps and trucks advancing on Coutances through a badly damaged village following a fierce bombardment.

BELOW: A page from the aircraft recognition leaflet issued to US troops to help ensure quick differentiation between friend and foe.

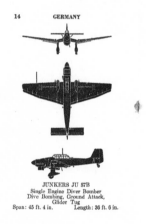

The bombing was dogged by misfortune. Although the attack was postponed because of bad weather on 24 July some bombers struck anyway, and several Americans were killed or wounded. On the following day the bombers came again, and this time 111 Americans were killed and another 490 wounded. Although the bombing had clearly rattled the defence, the initial infantry attacks still ran into firm resistance. However, General Collins believed that the Germans were shaken enough for him to commit his armour, and though the situation on 26 July "did not appear too bright" he did just that. Collins' instincts were correct, and by the end of the day one of his divisional commanders exulted: "This thing has busted wide open." There was indeed a jagged breach in the German defences, and Kluge had too little armour to counter-attack.

Bradley's success lay as much in what followed Cobra as in the battle itself. Recognizing that the Germans could no longer furnish a cohesive defence, he issued orders on 28 July for exploitation of the initial breakthrough. The results were impressive. The Americans reached Avranches on 30 July, and on the following day they seized the little bridge over the River Sélune at Pontaubault just before the Germans arrived to destroy it. Kluge admitted that "It's a madhouse here", and acknowledged that his whole left flank had collapsed.

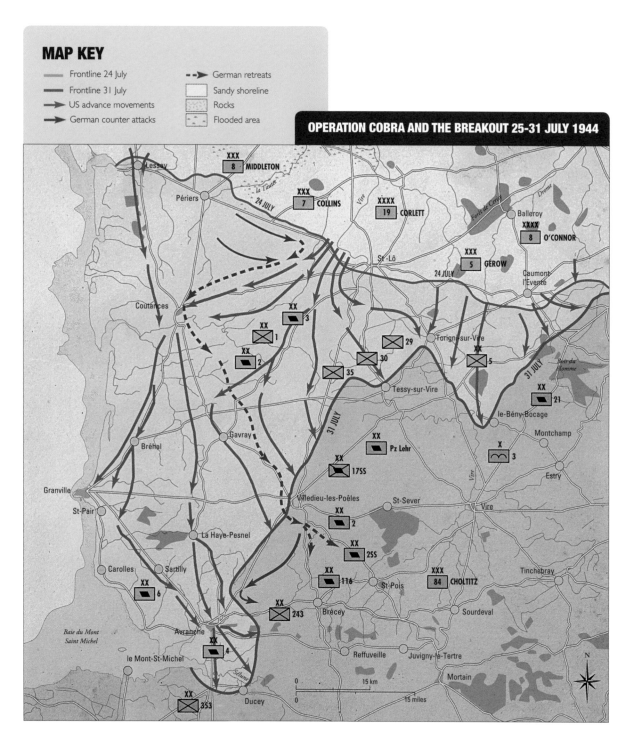

MAP KEY

- Frontline 24 July
- Frontline 31 July
- US advance movements
- German counter attacks
- German retreats
- Sandy shoreline
- Rocks
- Flooded area

OPERATION COBRA AND THE BREAKOUT 25-31 JULY 1944

On 1 August, with tanks of 4th Armoured Division rattling past Pontaubault towards Brittany, the Americans activated their new command structure, with Bradley stepping up to command 12th Army Group, Lieutenant General Courtney H. Hodges taking over First Army and Lieutenant General George S. Patton assuming command of the newly formed US Third Army. Eisenhower declared that Montgomery would remain ground force commander until SHAEF arrived in France and he assumed personal command. Although there was still much hard fighting to be done, Cobra had changed the pattern of the campaign.

OPERATION LÜTTICH

Hitler persistently intervened in the conduct of military operations. Sometimes he was right: his decision to stand fast in the face of the Russian counter-attack in December 1941, for instance, was well judged.

But by August 1944 his grip on reality had been severely eroded, and the unsuccessful assassination attempt of 20 July had increased his paranoia towards the General Staff. The decision to mount Operation Lüttich, the Mortain counter-attack, was his. On the face of things it was not wholly foolish. Exploitation after Cobra had left the Americans with a narrow corridor between Mortain and the coast, and it was not inconceivable that this could be cut, leaving Patton's divisions to the south dangerously short of fuel and supplies. But while Kluge and his staff recognized that a counter-attack could buy time, perhaps enough to fall back to a new defence line, Hitler envisaged something wholly different: a massive counter-stroke which would reverse his fortunes in the west and, as he put it, throw the Allies into the sea.

The Mortain counter-attack laboured under many disadvantages: several senior German commanders were markedly lacking in enthusiasm, and most participating units were already under-strength. However, in one respect Hitler's luck held. The weather on 7 August, when the battle began, was poor, grounding Allied fighter-bombers. And if Bradley had brief warning of the attack, produced

ABOVE: A company of Tiger II tanks, part of an SS Panzer division, camouflaged near Mortain on the eve of Operation Lüttich.

LEFT: US 30th Division

by Ultra, for some units on the ground the sudden appearance of numerous determined Germans came as a very unpleasant shock. Mortain itself had only just been occupied by the veteran US 30th Division, and although it was driven out of the town, the dominant Hill 317, just to the east, was held by part of an infantry battalion with artillery observers in "one of the outstanding small unit achievements in the course of the campaign." When the weather

ABOVE: Soft-skinned vehicles were hideously vulnerable to attack from the air.

BELOW: The Panther tank, with a 75mm gun, was developed by the Germans to counter the threat posed by the Soviet T-34. The Americans and British first encountered it in significant numbers in Normandy.

cleared the observers were able to direct fire onto the main road to the coast, just below them, and USAAF Thunderbolts and RAF Typhoons arrived to lacerate the attackers. Despite there being some early progress, the attack was going nowhere.

Hitler remained convinced that the offensive could have succeeded if it had been heavier, and ordered Eberbach, removed from command of 5th Panzer Army and given a scratch headquarters specifically for the new attack, to try again on 11 August. Eberbach soon recognized that he had too few tanks for the task, and Allied air superiority meant that they could only move while early-morning mist grounded aircraft. And Kluge could see that things were coming unstitched elsewhere: the Canadians were pushing hard down the Caen-Falaise road, and further south the Americans were cutting up from Le Mans towards Alençon. By continuing to strike westwards, the Germans were putting their heads further into the noose, and on 11 August Hitler authorized Eberbach to disengage, although, hopelessly unrealistically, he still hoped to try again later.

> "Tanks are the backbone of our defence, when they are withdrawn, our front will give way. If, as I foresee, this plan does not succeed, catastrophe is inevitable."
>
> **Field Marshal Gunther von Kluge, Commander in Chief West**

GUNTHER VON KLUGE

Von Kluge an army commander from 1939 to 1940, and promoted to field marshal after victory in France. Injured in Russia in 1943, he was re-employed in 1944 as Commander in Chief West, replacing Rundstedt on 3 July. Initially full of enthusiasm, he speedily concluded that his position was hopeless. Ordered to Germany in the wake of the 20 July assassination plot, he took poison on 19 August. His last letter spoke of shame at his failure but of continuing loyalty to Adolf Hitler.

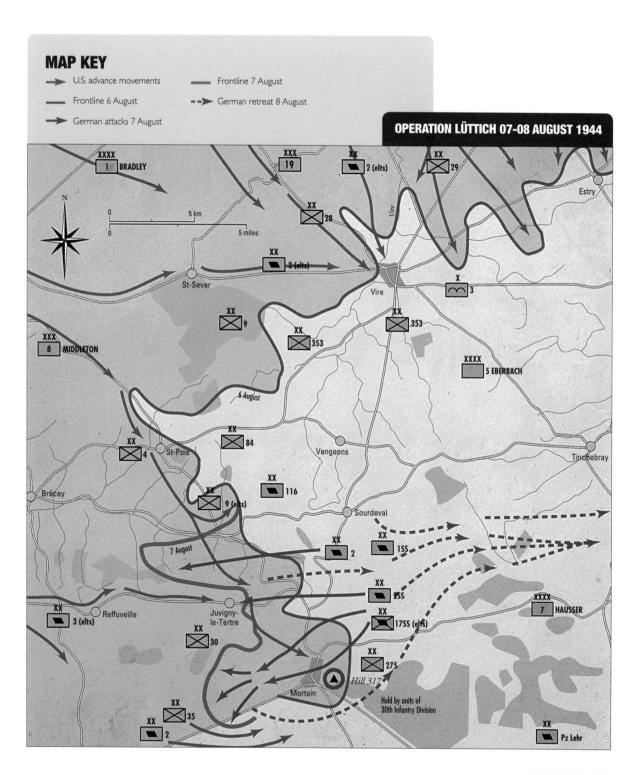

MAP KEY

→ U.S. advance movements

── Frontline 6 August

➤ German attacks 7 August

── Frontline 7 August

-‑►► German retreat 8 August

OPERATION LÜTTICH 07-08 AUGUST 1944

XXXX
1 BRADLEY

XXX
19

XX
2 (elts)

XX
29

Estry

N

0   5 km
0   5 miles

XX
28

Vire

XX
2 (elts)

St-Sever

X
3

XXX
8 MIDDLETON

XX
9

XX
353

XX
353

XXXX
5 EBERBACH

6 August

XX
84

Vengeons

Tinchebray

XX
4   St-Pois

Brécey

XX
9 (elts)

XX
116

Sourdeval

XX
1SS

7 August

XX
2

XX
SS

XXXX
7 HAUSSER

XX
3 (elts)   Reffuveille

Juvigny-
le-Tertre

XX
17SS (elts)

XX
30

XX
275

▲ *Hill 317*

Mortain

Held by units of
30th Infantry Division

XX
35

XX
2

XX
Pz Lehr

TACTICAL AIR SUPPORT

The Allies enjoyed air superiority throughout the campaign. The Luftwaffe had been weakened before D-Day by losses in combat and the effects of bombing on the German industrial base.

Indeed, the erosion of the Luftwaffe's fighter strength was one of the by-products of the strategic bombing campaign. It became harder to train pilots, and by 1944 German air power was in a descending spiral which could have only one result. German soldiers lived with the constant threat of air attack: they joked darkly that the "Normandy look" was an upward stare that gave a man a crick in his neck, and photographs and newsreels reveal constant emphasis on camouflage.

Yet if air power made a crucial contribution to Allied victory, it was not decisive in itself. Armies and air forces were not always comfortable bedfellows. The "bomber barons", like Carl Spaatz and Ira Eaker in the USAAF and Arthur Harris in the RAF, believed that their heavy bombers should be used against strategic targets in Germany, not tactical targets in Normandy, and the experience of Goodwood and Cobra confirmed them in this view. Even at a lower level, where air power was tactical in function, its effectiveness was limited by personality clashes. Air Marshal Coningham of Second Tactical Air Force cordially detested Montgomery, and Tedder, Eisenhower's deputy, sympathized with him. In contrast, Air Vice Marshal Harry Broadhurst, who supported Dempsey's Second Army, got on well with soldiers. So too did USAAF Major General Elwood R. "Pete" Quesada, whose IX Tactical Air Command supported Bradley. He not only enjoyed an excellent working relationship with Bradley himself, but persuaded him to put aircraft radios into tanks to improve communication between ground and air.

Communication was itself a major difficulty, and one of the reasons why Goodwood made limited progress was that the one forward air

ABOVE: A rocket-armed RAF Typhoon taking off from a forward airstrip. Aircraft were refuelled and rearmed on these strips, enjoying longer "loiter time" over the battlefield than if they had to return to Britain after each mission.

BELOW: Marauder medium bombers of the US 9th Air Force attacking German units moving up to the battlefront by road.

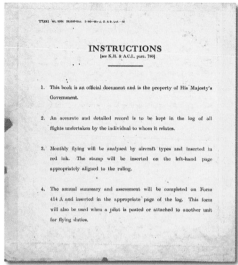

RIGHT: The logbook of a British Typhoon pilot, Flying Officer Henry "Poppa" Ambrose of 175 Squadron (whose motto was "Stop at Nothing"), detailing his ground support sorties from 8 to 31 August 1944.

controller on the main axis of the advance was in an unarmoured vehicle which was knocked out early on. It was rarely enough to target air attacks on a particular area: pilots had a better chance of success if a forward air controller could give them last minute directions, perhaps with a smoke shell to mark the target. Next, the limitations of the weapons in use limited the effectiveness of air attacks. Infantry and soft-skinned vehicles could be dealt with by machine-gun or cannon fire, but tanks were harder to destroy, and rockets, like those used by RAF Typhoons, lacked accuracy when used against moving armour. Even when the skies cleared over Mortain, and the flail of Allied air power was applied relentlessly, more tanks were abandoned by their terrified crews than were actually destroyed by rockets. Bad weather often made flying impossible, and "loiter time" over the battlefield was all too short until sufficient aircraft were based on temporary airstrips in France.

ABOVE: Canadians pause on their way to Falaise as Allied bombs fall just ahead of them.

ABOVE LEFT: Smoke and debris rising from a German ammunition dump hit by an air attack north of Falaise in mid-July.

Lastly, the Germans were adept at generating comprehensive ground-based air defence, with 88mm guns reaching up for high-flying aircraft and lighter weapons taking a toll of lower targets. Second Tactical Air Force and UK-based Fighter Command units between them lost 829 aircraft and over 1,000 aircrew killed or missing, and for the campaign as a whole the USAAF lost an average of 34 men and eight aircraft, and the RAF 36 men and nine aircraft, for every thousand sorties. There were times when the efforts of Allied pilots were not appreciated by men slogging it out on the ground, but the skies over Normandy were anything but safe.

HARRY BROADHURST

Commissioned into the RAF in 1926, Broadhurst quickly established a reputation as a skilled pilot and fine marksman. Heavily involved in the 1940 campaign and the Battle of Britain, he took over the Western Desert Air Force in January 1943 as the RAF's youngest air vice marshal. In 1944–45 he commanded a group in 2nd Tactical Air Force under Sir Arthur Coningham. He enjoyed Montgomery's confidence, and worked well with him during the campaign.

OPERATIONS TOTALIZE & TRACTABLE

In the wake of Goodwood, Lieutenant General Guy Simonds' II Canadian Corps assumed responsibility for the offensive towards Falaise, and in the process landed two heavy blows on the Germans, Operation Totalize on 7–10 August and Tractable on 14–16 August.

Although the rolling countryside crossed by the Caen-Falaise road was well suited to defence based on the long reach of the 88mm gun, Simonds planned to minimize its effectiveness by attacking with infantry at night, pushing armour through once the defence was breached. Heavy bombers would support the attacks, and artillery, which had grown in strength and effect as the campaign had developed, would crash out ahead of the advancing troops.

One of the lessons of Goodwood was that unprotected infantry found it hard to co-operate effectively with tanks in open country. Simonds accordingly decided to put much of his infantry into extemporized armoured personnel carriers, from which they would dismount only to attack their objectives. These vehicles were created by removing the guns, seats and ammunition bins from Priest self-propelled guns. Steel sheets were welded across the openings, and as armour plate was in short supply it was improvised by putting a thin layer of sand between sheets of mild steel. The new vehicles were known as "holy rollers" or "unfrocked priests". To help the armoured columns, moving in tight formation on the axis of the main road,

ABOVE Canadian infantry in half-tracks advance on Falaise. The white star on the vehicles was an Allied recognition symbol.

ABOVE: British 51st Highland Infantry Division

ABOVE: Canadian 2nd Armoured Brigade

GUY SIMONDS

Simonds was commissioned into the Canadian permanent force between the wars, and was Chief of Staff of I Canadian Corps before taking command of 1st Canadian Infantry Division in Sicily. He led II Canadian Corps in Normandy, and after the war became Chief Instructor of the Imperial Defence College, Commandant of the Canadian National Defence College and finally Chief of the Canadian General Staff. Simonds was temperamental, but set high standards, and was one of the best Allied corps commanders.

keep their direction in the dark, there were to be navigational aids like light anti-aircraft guns firing tracer ammunition in the direction of advance and radio direction beams.

Simonds' corps, comprising 2nd and 3rd Canadian Infantry Divisions, 4th Canadian Armoured Division and 2nd Canadian Armoured Brigade, was reinforced by the British 51st Highland Division and 33rd Armoured Brigade, and by 1st Polish Armoured Division. The bombing support for Tractable began at 11.00 on the night of 7 August, and the attacking columns moved forward shortly afterwards. There were useful gains during the night, and after dawn Polish and Canadian tanks moved through the infantry, getting as far as Cintheaux, a total advance of six or seven miles. Subsequent progress, against a hardening defence, was less impressive, and the attack paused on

ABOVE: Canadian infantry clearing a village on the way to Falaise. The second soldier is a sniper.

BELOW: Canadians pass destroyed vehicles on the Caen-Falaise road.

10 June. Operation Tractable followed a similar pattern, though the first attacks were in daylight, with medium bombers going in at 11.30 on the morning of 14 August and heavies following in the afternoon. The attackers were soon across the little River Laizon, and despite some inaccurate bombing and predictably stiff resistance, the infantry of 2nd Canadian Division had taken Falaise by midnight on 16 August. Not only did Totalize and Tractable result in the capture of this important objective, but they helped disorganize German plans for an offensive against the Americans. It was small wonder that Hitler admitted that 15 August was the worst day of his life.

MAP KEY

——— Front line 7 August
——— Front line 11 August
——— Front line 15 August
——— German defence zone

✳ Night bomber targets 7 August
✳ Day bomber targets 8 August
✳ Saturation bombing prior to attack

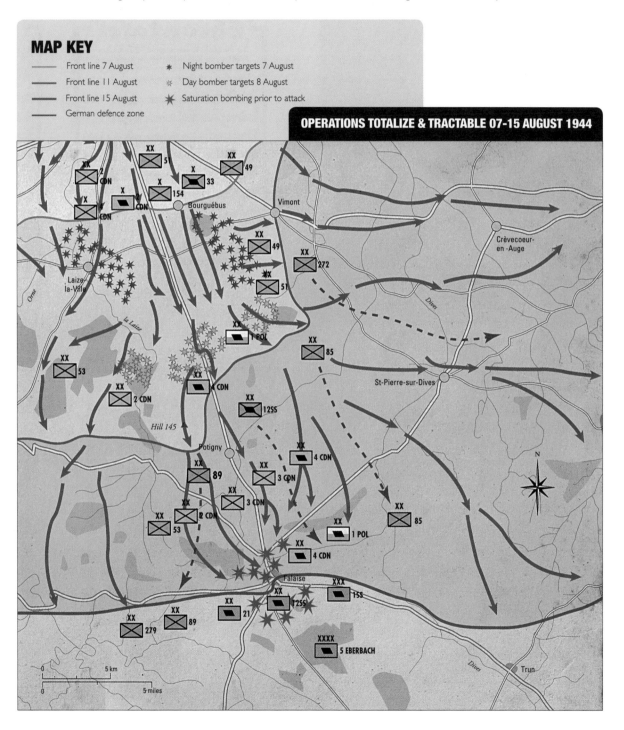

OPERATIONS TOTALIZE & TRACTABLE 07-15 AUGUST 1944

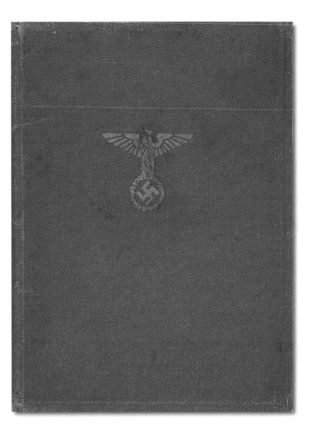

RIGHT: The Nazi Party membership book of Kurt "Panzer" Meyer, who joined the SS in 1933. In 1944, at the age of 33, he commanded the 12th SS Panzer Division Hitlerjugend in the Caen sector.

KURT "PANZER" MEYER

Meyer joined the SS in 1933, and fought in Poland before earning the Knight's Cross in Crete in 1941. In 1944, at the age of 33, he commanded the 12th SS Panzer Division Hitlerjugend in the Caen sector. He was a tough and resolute man. Driving up the Caen-Falaise road at the beginning of Operation Totalize, he found infantry streaming back in panic. He stood in the middle of the road and rallied them, ensuring that their positions around Cintheaux were held. After the war a Canadian tribunal sentenced him to death for the murder of prisoners. The sentence was commuted, and he was released in 1954, dying shortly afterwards.

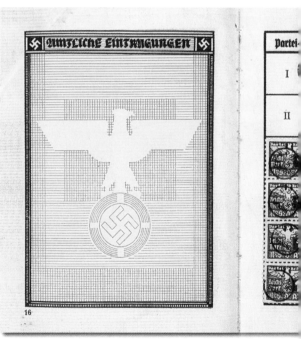

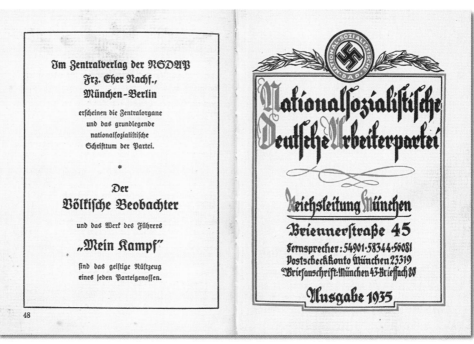

THE FALAISE POCKET

The battle of the Falaise Pocket was improvised in response to Allied successes and German failure. Both Montgomery and Bradley were quick to spot the chance offered them.

BELOW: Allied armour operating in the Falaise sector.

Bradley told the visiting Henry Morgenthau, US Treasury Secretary, that: "This is an opportunity that comes to a commander not more than once in a century. We are about to destroy an entire German army." The Allies had two major options, a "short hook" to create a pocket near Falaise, or a "long hook" to the Seine to achieve greater encirclement. Both were more difficult and more risky than they appear in hindsight, for an unplanned envelopment by two national army groups presented extraordinary problems of co-ordination. Moreover, though the German army was indeed beaten, some of its components still displayed their old aggressiveness, and were to show every determination of breaking any Allied ring at its weakest point.

"Forty-eight hours after the closing of the gap I was conducted through it on foot, to encounter scenes that could only be described by Dante. It was literally possible to walk for hundreds of yards at a time, stepping on nothing but dead and decaying flesh."

General Dwight D. Eisenhower

DAVID CURRIE

Currie was a Saskatchewan mechanic before joining the Canadian army. Commissioned from the ranks, he was commanding a squadron of the 29th Canadian Armoured Reconnaissance Regiment (South Alberta Regiment) by July 1944. In August he took St-Lambert-sur-Dives, on a German withdrawal route through the Falaise Pocket, and held it in the face of fierce attacks, earning the first Canadian VC of the campaign. He survived the war, and later became sergeant at arms in the Canadian parliament.

A telephone conversation between Bradley and Montgomery on 8 August established the short hook as the preferred option: Bradley's men would jab north towards Argentan, forming the lower jaw of a vice which would meet the British and Canadians jaw crunching down from Caen. Bradley halted his leading corps, Third Army's XV, just south of Argentan on 13 August, arguing that it was "better to have a solid shoulder at Argentan than a broken neck at Falaise". He was across

OPPOSITE: The debris of defeat near Chambois in the Falaise Pocket. Not all the dead in the Pocket were combatants. Chambois alone lost 17 inhabitants.

LEFT: US XV Corps

BELOW: German transport destroyed by artillery fire. Many combatants found the numerous dead horses in the Pocket particularly depressing.

WAR DIARY
or
INTELLIGENCE SUMMARY
(Delete heading not required).

Instructions regarding War Diaries and Intelligence Summaries are contained in F.S. Regs., Vol. I. Monthly War Diaries will be enclosed in A.F. C.2119. If this is not available, and for Intelligence Summaries, the cover will be prepared in manuscript.

Month and Year ...... Sierpień 1944.r.

Unit ...... 10.BRYGADA KAWALERII PANCERNEJ

Army Form **C. 2118.**

Commanding Officer ...PŁK.DYPL. MAJEWSKI.T.....

Place	Date	Hour	Summary of Events and Information	References to Appendices
Pole walki	20	0700	~~Rozpoznanie własnych~~ Ugrupowanie Brygady wzg. 262 obsadzone przez 1. i 2. Pułki Panc oraz 8 Baon Strzelców. 10.Pułk Drag. trzyma PLC skraj CHAMBOIS 2.Ułanów 1.klm. od CHAMBOIS /PŁC-WSCH./.	
		0800	1.Panc. odpiera potężne natarcie czołgów wspartych wielką ilością piechoty. /straty własne i NPLA ~~bardzo~~ duże/.	
		0810	2. oraz 10.Pułk Dragonów wykonuje przeciwnatarcie na czołgi i piechotę NPLA które wyszło z rej. ST. LAMBERT SUR DIVES. Npl.wycofał się.	
		10.40	10.Drag. odpiera nacicierające /"Kampfgruppen" chcące przebić się przez CHAMBOIS.	
		1050	1.Panc. odpiera 2 natarcia czołgów i piechoty. ~~W związku z tym~~ Pomimo rozkazu Dcy Brygady nakazującego wycofanie się ze względu na ciężką sytuację pułku 1.Panc. walczy dalej i utrzymuje teren.	
		1540	10.Drag. zużył 70 % amunicji. Dowóz zaopatrzenia niemożliwy.	
		1709	2.Panc. walczy z silnym ugrupowaniem Panter i ponosi duże straty we współdziałającej piechocie.	
		1725	Ogień art. zatrzymuje natarcie NPLA na 440568.	
		1740	Nowe natarcie czołgów NPLA na 2.Panc. z rej. 450550.	szkic 1
		1805	2.Panc. dostaje rozkaz do wycofania się na las.	
		1815	2.Panc. czołgi NPLA wdarły się w pierwsze linie.	
		1850	NPL wycofał się z rej 2.Panc.	
		2035	Meldunek 1.Panc. o krytycznej sytuacji.	
		2025	2.Panc. otrzymał pomoc Kanadyjczyków.	
		2125	1.Panc. odciążony działaniem Kanadyjczyków.	
			Załącznik - meldunki plik.	Zał. Nr. 1.
			Notatki ofic.takt.	Zał. Nr. 2.

DOWÓDCA BRYGADY

MAJEWSKI DOWÓDCA BRYGADY
płk dypl.

Wt.34863/1676 800,000 11/43 W. H. & S. 51-7675

---

the boundary into 21st Army Group's area, Eberbach's armour was still threatening, and he was uncertain whether there were enough Germans in the Pocket to make the operation worthwhile. Bradley later complained that Montgomery's caution delayed closing the gap, but it is fair to say that neither commander (nor indeed Eisenhower himself) displayed that killer instinct which would have enabled them to close the gap sooner. Nor ought we to be surprised. These were the armies of mighty democracies nearing the end of a long war, with a chain of command that reflected national and personal tensions.

Early on 16 August Kluge recommended evacuation of the salient, and had begun to withdraw before formal permission reached him later that day. It was his last act as a commander, for Field Marshal Walther Model arrived to relieve him on 17 August. As the Germans began to pull back, Bradley, following a phone conversation with Montgomery, ordered Patton to seize Chambois: the jaws of the vice were inching shut. By the evening of 18 August there was still a gap of three miles between the Americans and the Polish armoured division, on the extreme south-east edge of Mongomery's thrust, but on 19 August Americans and Poles met in Chambois. There was still some very sharp fighting. Major David Currie of the South Alberta Regiment earned the Victoria

ABOVE: A page from the official war diary of the 10th Brigade of the 1st Polish Armoured Division detailing its action in closing the Falaise Gap on 20 August.

RIGHT: Polish Armoured 1st Division.

Cross in St-Lambert-sur-Dives, and the Poles, on what they called "The Mace" above Chambois, fought desperately to keep Germans in the Pocket and to prevent units outside from boring an escape hole.

When the battle ended on 21 August the killing fields of the Pocket, repeatedly strafed by Allied aircraft, resembled, as Eisenhower put it, something out of Dante's *Inferno*, where it was difficult to walk without treading on human flesh. Although, as subsequent critics pointed out, greater destruction could have been wrought had the Pocket been sealed sooner, it was the culmination of a defeat of shocking proportions. In the previous ten weeks the defenders of Normandy had lost some 1,300 tanks, at least 50,000 dead, and 200,000 prisoners.

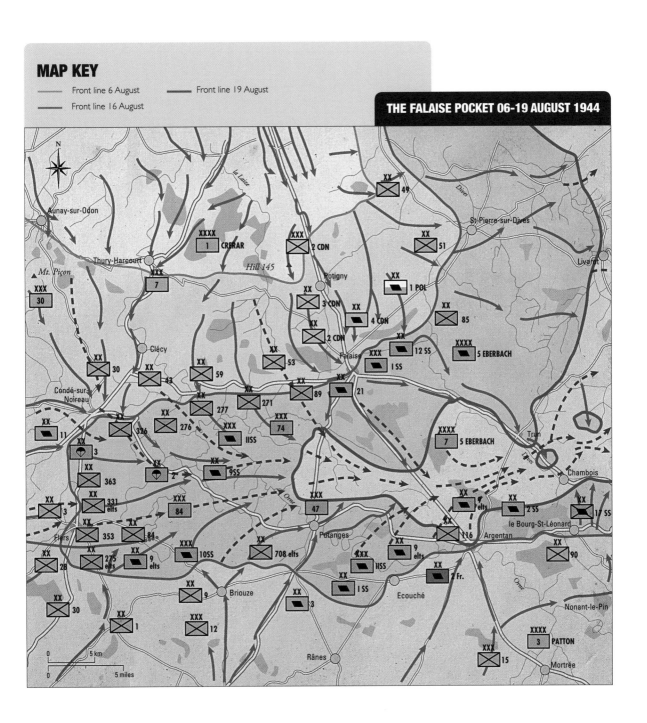

MAP KEY

— Front line 6 August
— Front line 16 August
— Front line 19 August

THE FALAISE POCKET 06-19 AUGUST 1944

N

Aunay-sur-Odon

la Laize

XX 46

Dives

St-Pierre-sur-Dives

XXXX 1 CRERAR

XXX 2 CDN

XX 51

Livarot

Thury-Harcourt

Hill 145

Mt. Piçon

XXX 7

Potigny

XX 1 POL

XXX 30

XXX 3 CDN

XX 4 CDN

XX 85

XX 2 CDN

XXXX 5 EBERBACH

Clécy

XX 30

XX 53

Falaise

XX 12 SS

XXX 1 SS

XX 59

XXX 1 SS

Condé-sur-Noireau

XX 43

XX 89

XX 21

XX 11

XX 277

XX 271

XXXX 7 5 EBERBACH

Trun

XX 3

XX 326

XX 276

XXXX 1ISS

XXX 74

Dives

Chambois

XX 363

XX 2

XX 9SS

XXX 47

XX elts

XX 2 SS

XX 17 SS

XX 3

XX 331 elts

XXX 84

Orne

XX elts

le Bourg-St-Léonard

XX 3

XX 353

XX 84

Putanges

XX 116

Argentan

XX 28

XX 275 elts

XX 9 elts

XXX 10SS

XX 708 elts

XXX 9 elts

XX 90

XX 1ISS

Ecouché

XX 30

XX 9

Briouze

XX 3

XX 1 SS

XX 2 Fr.

Orne

Nonant-le-Pin

XX 1

XXX 12

XXXX 3 PATTON

Rânes

XXX 15

Mortrée

0 5 km
0 5 miles

THE LIBERATION OF PARIS

The Americans struck out for the Seine before fighting had finished at Falaise. On 19 August they crossed the river near Mantes, and the British crossed at Vernon five days later.

BELOW: Battle in the shadow of the Arc de Triomphe. Soldiers of the French 2nd Armoured Division look out across German dead on the Champs Elysées.

Hitler still hoped to hold Paris, but Model pointed out that the city's retention would be "a big military problem" and knew that there was little chance of holding it with the forces at his disposal.

The Paris Resistance had views of its own. Although de Gaulle sent an emissary with instructions to avoid any "premature rising", on 19 August policemen hoisted the tricoleur above the Prefecture of Police, and there was soon sporadic fighting. The military commander of Paris, Lieutenant General Dietrich von Choltitz, planned to defend the southern and western suburbs, but was told to prepare for demolition the city's public utilities, bridges and many of its most famous buildings. Choltitz was an honourable man with no appetite for this, but had a family in Germany and needed to find a solution that would neither destroy Paris nor result in "premature" surrender.

On 20 August Choltitz agreed to a short-lived truce, and a flurry of Resistance emissaries to the Allies resulted in Eisenhower's agreement that the Free French 2nd Armoured Division under Major General Philippe Leclerc, which had arrived in France on 1 August,

PHILIPPE LECLERC

Wounded and captured in 1940, Leclerc escaped and joined de Gaulle in Britain, was sent to equatorial Africa (with a nom de guerre to protect his family), and led a column across the Sahara to join the British 8th Army in Libya. He commanded 2nd Armoured Division, the first Allied unit to enter Paris, in 1944–45, and was French representative at the Japanese surrender. Killed in a 1947 plane crash, Leclerc was posthumously created Marshal of France.

would drive straight for Paris. When Leclerc received the order his men were still 120 miles away, but he reached Rambouillet, where he met de Gaulle, on 23 August. They agreed that Leclerc should edge eastwards to find the least-defended route into the city, and at 9.30 on the evening of 24 August his three leading tanks drew up outside the Town Hall. On the next day there was a last burst of fighting, with moments of terrible poignancy as French soldiers died close to home, before Choltitz surrendered. On 26 August Charles de Gaulle walked ahead of his generals and a great crowd for a Te Deum at Notre Dame. There was sniping on the way, but his step never faltered.

As Paris revelled in its liberation the Allied armies hurtled across France. On 1 September Eisenhower assumed command of ground forces, but for the moment he had little impact as his divisions rolled across the battlefields of the First World War, and over the Marne and the Somme, on which Hitler briefly hoped to make a stand. The German divisions which had escaped from

LEFT: A Frenchwoman exults as the tricoleur is raised in Paris.

BELOW: Parisians extend welcoming hands to US troops entering the city on 25 August.

Normandy were still too badly bruised to fight. Although those of Army Group G, dislodged by an Allied invasion of the Riviera on 15 August, were in better shape, even Walther Model, "Führer's Fireman" though he was, could not make a stand till he neared the borders of Germany.

Montgomery had always thought in terms of crossing the Seine in D+90 days, and had indeed achieved it. He was wrong to maintain that things had gone according to plan: few campaigns do, and that in Normandy was no exception. It is unfortunate that the tensions inherent in the alliance were magnified as leaders wrote their memoirs and attracted biographers. The real truth of Normandy was that the forces of a mighty coalition had entered the continent of Europe and, mistakes notwithstanding, struck a telling blow at its occupiers. They deserve our gratitude.

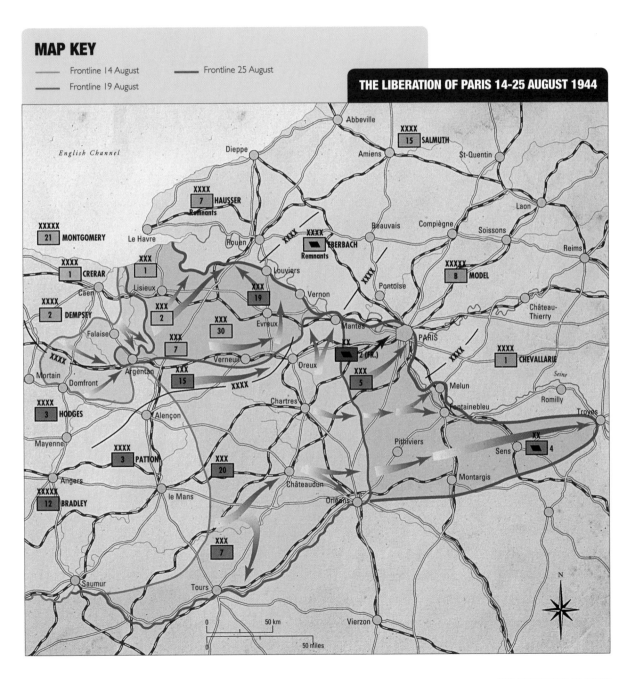

MAP KEY

—— Frontline 14 August   —— Frontline 25 August

—— Frontline 19 August

THE LIBERATION OF PARIS 14-25 AUGUST 1944

INDEX

Page numbers in bold type refer to autobiographical entries or to maps.

CREDITS

Imperial War Museums photographs

A vast majority of photographs reproduced in the book have been taken from the collections of the Photograph Archive at Imperial War Museums. The Museum's reference numbers for each of the photographs are listed below, giving the page on which they appear in the book and any location indicator (t-top, b-bottom, l-left, r-right, m-middle).

I: B 5103 (m); 7: TR 1629 (t); 10: HU 1904 (mr); 13: CH 14706 (tc); HU 3059 (br); TR 1042 (tr); 17: MH 24327 (b); 20: HU 3056; 23: H 42527; 24: H 42529 (tr); E (MOS) 1451 (bl); 25: H 42531 (t); H 42535 (tr); 27: AP 30390; 28: B 9376 (bl); 30: EA 34007 (t); KY 24324 (b); 31: HU 16541 (t); 33: MH 24891; 34: B 5233; 37: MH 24891; 39: CL 26 (t); 40: H 39070 (t); H 39074 (br); B 5291 (bl); 43: EA 25509 (t); 49: 23: HU 73228; 50: AP 26001 (tr); EA 25902 (b); 53: AP 25625 (b); 56: EA 25641; 56: MH 24806 (br); 57: MH 24806; 63: OWIL 44977 (br); 67: B 5245; 69: B 5218; 70: HU 2001 (br) 71: B 5685; 73: 30MH 4505; 74: A 23938 (t); HU 91241; 76: B 5228 (t); MH 3097 (br); 79: B 5103; 81: 11791 (tr); B 5114 (b); 82: MH 2011 (ml); B 7370 (br); 85: CL 344; 86: MH 7887 (r); 88: B 86333; 91: B 5742; 92: EA 5036 (t); T 54 (b); 93: EA 45245a; 97: A 24832 (tr); MH 2405 (b); 99: B 5950 (t); B 5957 (br); 100: B 10600 (tr); B 5963 (br); 103: AP 282111; 104: OWIL 27887 (tr); KY 27786 (b); 106: PL 28033; 107: EA 27890; 109: CL 61; 110: ZZZ 12016E; 112: B 6897 (br); 114: B 6800; 115: B 6794; 117: OWIL 30273 (t); EA 30750 (br); 118: EA 25979 (t); 119: B 5802 (t); EA 26521 (b); 123: EA 30511; 125: EA 30445 (b); 127: CL 477; 128: TP 11296E (tl); B 7407 (br); 131: KY 31764 (t); 132: KY 31774 (tr); 132: PL 31235 (bl); 139: CL 147 (t); 141: LNA 52456 (tl); NYP 36636 (tr); CH 13092 (br); 143: HU 52362 (t); A 17963 (br); 144: NYT 4974 (t); HU 91226 (b); 149: NYP 37818 (t); 150: EA 34532; 151: HU 62168 (t); MH 4204 (b); 155: EA 37079 (t); OWIL 33584 (br); 156: OWIL 35967 (tr); EA 35146 (b)

Photographs from sources outside Imperial War Museums with the kind permission of:

AKG-London: 18 (m)

Associated Press: US Signal Corps: 3, 60

Bildarchiv Preußischer Kulturbesitz: 19 (b); 86 (bl); 89 (tr); 135; 136 (tr)

Penny Howard Bates, daughter of Major John Howard D.S.O., C.de G., from his archives: 35 (tr); 37

Library of Congress: 53 (t)

Magnum Photos: Robert Capa: 59

Memorial Pegasus, Avenue de Major Howard, 14860 Ranville, Normandie, France: 118 (mr)

Musée Airborne, 14 rue Eisenhower, 50480 Ste-Mère-Eglise, Normandie, France: 119 (tr)

Musée D-Day Omaha, Rte de Grandcamp, 14710 Vierville-sur-Mer, Normandie, France: 24 (br); 28 (tr); 30 (ml); 107 (t)

Musée du Débarquement, Utah Beach, 50480 Sainte Marie du Mont, Normandie, France. (The permanent exposition in the museum comes from private donations.): 50 (b); 52 (ml, tr)

The National D-Day Museum, New Orleans: 44 (mr)

The Tank Museum, Bovington, UK: 131 (br)

Ullstein Bild: 13 (bl); 18 (br); 101 (tr); 136 (br)

US National Archives: back cover photo; 1 (background photo); 2-3 (background photo); 13 (tl); 43 (br); 44 (br); 52 (tl); 54 (tr); 63 (tr); 125 (tr); 132 (tr); 136 (t); 139 (br)

All other badges and medals not credited were photographed by Carlton Books

Memorabilia printed on the page with the kind permission of:

Janet Ambrose: 140 (log book)

© Canadian War Museum (CWM): 75 (letter)

D-Day Museum, Portsmouth Museums & Records Service: 61 (Omaha Beach defences documents); 94-96 (early Mulberry designs)

Penny Howard Bates, daughter of Major John Howard D.S.O., C.de G., from his archives: 35, 36, 37 (Major John Howard's documents)

Imperial War Museums, Department of Documents: 95 (Churchill memo) Papers of Captain J. J. Youngs, 92/50/1; 146–147 (Nazi Party membership book) German Miscellaneous 153, Sweeting Collection

Imperial War Museums: 8/9 (German overview map) Heer Gen. St. d. H. Fremde Heere West, M.I.14/841; photographs of all medals and insignia, SHAEF envelope, 7, and Captain Vaughn's pistol, 34

Papers of The Rt Hon Viscount Montgomery of Alamein CMG CBE and the Imperial War Museum, Department of Documents: 83 (letter)

Memorial Pegasus, Avenue de Major Howard, 14860 Ranville, Normandie, France: 36 (letter); 112 (rectangular propaganda leaflets)

Musée Airborne, 14 rue Eisenhower, 50480 Ste-Mère-Eglise, Normandie, France: 10 (poster); 44 (hand-drawn map); 120–121 (diary)

Musée D-Day Omaha, Rte de Grandcamp, 14710 Vierville-sur-Mer, Normandie, France: 132 (aircraft recognition leaflet)

Musée du Débarquement, Place du 6-Juin, 14117 Arromanches, Normandie, France: 19 (beach defences); 62 (Information Team messages); 113 (first-aid leaflet)

Musée du Débarquement, Utah Beach, 50480 Ste-Marie-du-Mont, Normandie, France. (The permanent exposition in the museum comes from private donations.): 29 (Operation Hardtack 24 orders); 31 (leaflet); 46/47 (printed "jump" map); 53 (newspaper)

Musée du Mur de l'Atlantique, Le Grand Bunker, Avenue du 6 Juin, 14150 Ouistreham, Riva Bella, Normandie, France: 82 (German radio log sheet)

The Polish Institute and Sikorski Museum: 152 (1st Polish Armoured Division war diary)

Artworks

Ray Hutchins/Artech: 74, 89, 136

Specially commissioned maps © Cartographica Ltd: 5, 11, 21, 41, 45, 51, 58, 68, 77, 80, 87, 101, 105, 111, 124, 129, 133, 137, 145, 153, 157